PEACE AT THE CATHAY

PETER HIBBARD

A Century of International Hospitality
on the Bund

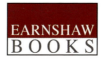

PEACE AT THE CATHAY
Peter Hibbard

ISBN-13: 978-988-16164-7-0

2013 © Peter Hibbard
Published by Earnshaw Books Ltd. (Hong Kong).

All rights reserved. No part of this book may be reproduced in material form, by any means, whether graphic, electronic, mechanical or other, including photocopying or information storage, in whole or in part. May not be used to prepare other publications without written permission from the publisher except in the case of brief quotations embodied in critical articles or reviews. For information contact info@earnshawbooks.com.

CONTENTS

Introduction	1
1. Boarding And Hoarding On The Bund	7
2. Shanghai's Palace	17
3. The House That Sassoon Built	33
4. Architectural Marvel	41
5. A New Era For Shanghai	53
6. The Cathay Sisters	67
7. Made To Order	87
8. Four-Minute Guests	97
9. Celebrities At The Cathay	109
10. On The Town	117
11. Champagne, Curfews, And Conflicts	135
12. Strangers In Shanghai	153
13. Peace At The Cathay	163
Cathay Tidbits	182
Hotel Directory For 1939	183
Architects And Contractors To Sassoon House	184
Bibliography	185

INTRODUCTION

In April 2007, the doors to Shanghai's famed Peace Hotel quietly closed, marking the end of an era that began a century earlier. The Palace Hotel, one of its two buildings, which partially opened in April 1907, went into full operation in 1909 upon the completion of its front section on Shanghai's legendary waterfront promenade, the Bund. The Palace Hotel took pride of place on its main intersection with Nanking Road and offered amenities and luxuries to compare with the best hotels throughout the world, promoting Shanghai's rise as Asia's most cosmopolitan, progressive and modern city.

Such was the frenzy of development in early 20th century Shanghai that it wasn't long before the hotel was remodelled to keep up with the fast-changing tastes of its residents and visitors. With the 1920s came the stately round-the-world cruise liners, a growing American presence and the Jazz Age. The Cathay Hotel, which would not have looked out of place in New York, opened opposite the Palace Hotel in 1929, signalling the dawn of a new age of opulence and luxury in a city besotted by glitz and glamour. Behind the venture was the legendary British Jewish businessman Sir Victor Sassoon, one of the wealthiest men in the world – and one who knew how to throw a real party.

The parties came to an end with the Japanese occupation of the city following Pearl Harbour in 1941, and though there was some cause for celebration after the end of the Pacific War in 1945, it was not long before the People's Liberation Army arrived in Shanghai in May 1949, altering the fate of two of the foremost foreign hotels in Asia. The Cathay Hotel reopened as the Peace

Opposite *The Peace Hotel in 2006*

Hotel in 1956 to accommodate a rising tide of visitors from Soviet Russia and the Eastern Bloc, and the Palace Hotel became its south building in 1965. Following China's opening to international tourism in 1978, the Peace Hotel etched out a new career, catering to those from around the world looking to capture the charm and decadence of a bygone age. Like its octogenarian jazz band, it soon became a legend. And today the two hotel buildings, yet again, herald a new era of opulence and luxury on the Bund, Shanghai's front door to the world. The former Palace Hotel opened as the Swatch Art Peace Hotel, and the former Cathay Hotel as the Fairmont Peace Hotel in 2010.

How different it was in the days when I first visited, and became enthralled by, the Peace Hotel in early 1986. There were few luxuries around, but crawling over every crevice and corridor of an institution cocooned in the past, I conjured up images of how it might have been in the heady days of the 1920s and 1930s, and departed with a determination to find out more about its illustrious past. This book draws heavily on research initiated in the late 1980s and early 1990s in Hong Kong, Shanghai, Beijing and the UK, resulting in a first draft in 1993. Material from that period, and from later research, has already been reproduced, in part, in a number of my publications, but my ambition for a book dedicated entirely to the Peace Hotel has now been realised 20 years on thanks to Graham Earnshaw of Earnshaw Books. New material on other historic hotels, which form part of the story of the hotel companies who operated the former Palace and Cathay hotels, has also been incorporated.

Peter Hibbard,
March 2013

Opposite *Design for Sassoon House incorporating the Cathay Hotel, 1928*

Below *Design for Sassoon House, 1925*

CATHAY

E. CARRARD
General Manager

TELEPHONE
11240

SHAN

Start the evening off pleasantly—and correctly—by stopping by for a cocktail at the place after eight... Dine and dance in the ballroom afterwards.

THE SILVER BAR 8TH FLOOR

THE CATHAY

4

1 BOARDING AND HOARDING ON THE BUND

OPIUM, OPIUM, OPIUM! The sweet smell of it had spawned fortunes for the British while spreading misery and rancour throughout China. It led to the Opium War of 1839 to 1842, which in turn allowed the British to build Shanghai as a base to expand their mercantile ambitions. The first settlers arriving after Captain Balfour, its first British Consul, declared the port open for trade in November 1843 and came looking for fortune. Few of them could have guessed at the bounty that would bloat their bellies within the space of a few short years.

Among the newcomers was the young Elias David Sassoon, fresh from Bombay. His father, David, a leading figure in the Mesopotamian (Iraqi) Jewish community and founder of David Sassoon & Co., had moved the family to India in 1832 to escape religious persecution in Baghdad. Though primarily a banking enterprise, his company made much of its fortune in the opium trade from India to southern China. And much greater riches were amassed in Shanghai, as the numbers of opium chests passing through its gateway swelled in the early 1850s.

The British established themselves in the area alongside the Whangpoo (Huangpu) River, developing its muddy foreshore into an esplanade they called the Bund – a term for a causeway or embankment adopted from India. By 1848, they had secured 460 acres of territory, known as the English Settlement, where foreigners could live under immunity from Chinese law. However, their hopes of maintaining it as an exclusive foreign area were disposed of with a tenacious sagacity as tens of thousands of Chinese sought sanctuary within its confines following the outbreak of the Taiping Rebellion (1850-1864). The British set about hastily constructing wooden dwellings in terraces, completely an anathema to Chinese ways, to maximise profits from the Chinese tenants packed in like sardines. One British landlord remarked that, 'it is my business to make a fortune within the least possible loss of time . . . and what can it matter to me if all Shanghai disappears

Opposite *Late 19th century postcard of the Central Hotel* (left) *and the premises of E. D. Sassoon* (right)

CENTRAL HOTEL,
SHANGHAI.
Established 1875.

ELECTRIC LIGHTING THROUGHOUT THE PREMISES.

TELEGRAPHIC ADDRESS:— "CENTRAL, SHANGHAI."

This long established SELECT Family Hotel, situated on the Bund, facing the River, in the centre of the Settlements, is now fitted with the latest Modern Improvements, including Bath and Dressing rooms ATTACHED to suites and single rooms, with Hot and Cold Water laid on, Douche, Shower sprays, etc., and heated to a comfortable temperature during winter.

Commodious Reception Room for Visitors.

Separate Rooms for Private Dinner Parties, &c.

Prime location on the Bund and Nanking Road intersections, 1880s

afterwards in fire or flood?' Trading in opium and in property, were the two sure-fire ways to make a fortune in Shanghai in the mid- to late-nineteenth century. And the Sassoons had more than their fair share of interest in both.

Drinking champagne by the crate was the order of the day and the profligacy of the times was expressed in a fine show of solid 'compradoric' style buildings, featuring wide verandas and circular columns, stretching along the Bund. In 1857, visiting American merchant George F. Train remarked that the commercial houses on and around the Bund 'entirely eclipse the humble residences of our commission

Opposite *Modern amenities on offer at the Central Hotel, 1880s*

Opening advert in the North-China Herald, *November 1875*

CENTRAL HOTEL,

Corner of Nanking Road and Bund, Shanghai,

WILL BE OPENED

On *WEDNESDAY, the 3rd NOVEMBER*, 1875.

THIS commodious First-Class HOTEL has been fitted up in a very superior manner, with every regard to the comfort of intending visitors

The DINING SALOON is most spacious and commands a full view of the Bund and River.

The BILLIARD ROOM is Furnished with English and American Tables and provided with a Bar stocked with the choicest Liquors only.

The Two Upper Floors comprise a Handsome GENERAL DRAWING ROOM, from which a splendid view of the Bund, River and surrounding Country can be obtained; PRIVATE DINING ROOMS, SUITES of APARTMENTS and DOUBLE and SINGLE BED ROOMS, with the necessary BATH ROOMS, &c.

The CUISINE is under the able direction of Monsieur VOLLHARDT, whose talents as a Chef have already been fully proved in Shanghai and elsewhere.

MEAL HOURS.

TIFFIN...At Noon.
DINNER ....From 6.30 to 8 P M.

Terms and full particulars can be obtained upon application to Mr. **F. E. REILLY**, at the office of the HOTEL.

n 6no 1377   Shanghai, 2nd November, 1875.

merchants in the West. Comfort is the first thought of the China merchant, and comfort is the second, and, I may safely add, comfort is the third. Money is only an auxiliary in catering to his wish.' It was on the Bund's principal intersection, at that time known as Park Lane, and later as Nanking (Nanjing) Road, that the Commercial Hotel replaced the Victoria Hotel in 1853.

The newly established Hongkong and Shanghai Banking Corporation leased part of its premises in 1865 and when it moved to more spacious offices further down the Bund, the building was torn down. It was replaced by the Central Hotel, which opened in November 1875 under the proprietorship of Mr. F. E. Reilly. Proud of its fine location, the hotel offered sedan chairs for hire, arranged up-country houseboat

Opposite *New lawns on the Bund in the mid-1880s, with Central Hotel to the left*

The Bund looking north, 1860s

trips, and boasted three billiard tables as well as the best wine cellar and European kitchen in Shanghai. The hotel featured a private dining room and bar on the ground floor; four residences, a two-room suite and a drawing-room above; and bedrooms on its top floor.

The Central Hotel provided a home away from home for foreign visitors, a refuge where China was thrown into the background. In 1877 a visiting secretary from the British Legation in Peking (Beijing) recounted that he was 'quite unprepared to find such a splendid town. If you can picture to yourself all the large London Clubs and some hundred of the finest city houses transferred to the Thames Embankment you will get an idea of the Bund. In the side streets there are shops similar to those of Bond Street but very much larger.' It was in the same year that Elias Sassoon, who had split from the family firm and founded E. D. Sassoon & Company in 1867, purchased the site opposite the Central Hotel on which Asia's finest hotel was to emerge six decades later – at a time when huge fortunes would yet again be made in property speculation.

To the delight of the editor of *North-China Daily News*, the local British newspaper, work on demolishing the buildings on the plot, previously occupied by Augustine Heard &

Co., began in March 1877, 'in place of which are to be built two hongs of a much more pretentious style of architecture.' The new Sassoon venture also allowed the widening and straightening of their Nanking Road frontage, which had been a 'source of continual inconvenience to traffic.' However, it would soon become a bottleneck again as rickshaws, Shanghai's taxis of the day, recently introduced from Japan, piled up outside the hotel. The hotel also instituted its own luxury taxi service in June 1877 when 'telegraphic communication' was established with the Shanghai Horse Bazaar Company, at the far end of Nanking Road. Guests were notified that horse-driven 'carriages of all descriptions' could be obtained at a few minutes' notice.

Jacob Sassoon, Elias's eldest son, who was living in the company's new premises, was not amused. In a letter of July 1879 to the Shanghai Municipal Council, the area's foreign legislative body, he complained that 'noisy' rickshaw pullers were keeping him awake until one or two in the morning, and pleaded for them to be restricted to the Bund outside the hotel. A contemporaneous account conveyed that:

the Bund is crowded at all hours of the day by foot passengers and vehicles. Neat broughams, victorias, dog carts, drawn by sleek Chinese ponies, and driven by Celestial coachmen in strange liveries, pass and repass; flocks of jin-ricshas, some running swiftly and smoothly along on spider wheels, hand-carts pushed by panting coolies, and the celebrated vehicle of China, the only one not imported by the foreigner – the passenger barrow, with seats arranged over the wheel like those of an Irish jaunting car, on which sometimes a whole family sits and is whirled gaily along by a muscular coolie.

CENTRAL HOTEL,
SHANGHAI.

*T*HIS long established SELECT Family Hotel, situated on the Bund, facing the River, in the Centre of the Settlements, has lately undergone Extensive Alterations, and is now fitted with the latest Modern Improvements, including Bath and Dressing-Rooms attached to Suites and Single Rooms, with Hot and Cold Water laid on, and heated to a Comfortable Temperature during Winter. Separate Rooms for Private Dinner Parties, etc.

The Hotel is Lighted throughout with the Electric Light.

An Assistant will attend on Passengers arriving by all Mail Steamers.

J. E. REILLY,
Proprietor.

N.B.—TELEGRAPHIC ADDRESS:
CENTRAL, SHANGHAI.

More home comforts on offer in 1893

For Sale, advert from the North-China Herald, *July 1879*

In that same month of July 1879, Mr. Reilly advertised that the 'goodwill, lease, furniture and fixtures' of the hotel were up for sale, but nothing came of it until July 1896 when a newly formed company known as the Central Stores Limited purchased the hotel. They immediately set about making improvements to the property, but, despite a sharp hike in tariffs, couldn't keep up with ever-increasing demand from new arrivals. The foreign population of the International Settlement – amalgamated from the former English and American Settlements in 1863 – shot up from around 4,400 in 1895 to 6,800 in 1900. Central Stores Limited reverted to purchasing buildings near the hotel to accommodate its stores business and extra rooms. By April 1897, 15 bedrooms and eight bathrooms had been added to the 30-room hotel. However, the improvements didn't impress a correspondent from *The Hotel World* magazine in 1898, who found the cuisine inferior and that, although the bedrooms were 'passable enough the lavatory and sanitary arrangements were not what would be desired.'

At the turn of the twentieth century, with the anti-foreign revolt, the 'Boxer Uprising,' in Peking, the hotel bar became a favoured haunt of foreign men-of-war, blue-jackets and marines. In October 1900, Messrs. E. D. Sassoon and Co., who were still not the happiest of neighbours, led a protest over the mayhem and noise created by drunken sailors. They received support from many of the British community, who perfunctorily penned letters to the *North-China Daily News* telling of 'shocking nuisances' and of the corner as being 'an impossible place for ladies.' The hotel management laid the blame on inadequate policing of rickshaw traffic. However, they did restrict liquor sales to naval officers only and converted the large bar into a reading room, dining room and buffet in 1901, when Mr. Campbell – formerly of the Club Hotel Yokohama and the Florence Hotel, Kandy in Ceylon – took over its management. He concluded that the hotel stood 'as second to none' in Shanghai, in terms of comfort and convenience. However, it still had to turn guests away as a new tide of tourists, travellers and settlers descended on Shanghai with the dawn of the new century, and thoughts turned towards offering more commodious accommodations.

Opposite *Cutting the Bund lawns, late 1880s, with Central Hotel and Sassoon premises in the middle of the picture*

2 | SHANGHAI'S PALACE

AN IMPRESSIVE SCHEME for replacing the Central Hotel with a larger building was outlined by the Central Stores Limited in January 1904. Work on the new hotel was to be staged in two sections, scheduled for completion before April 1906 and January 1908, respectively. The *North-China Herald* announced it as a 'sky-scraper, six-stories, 96 feet-high, the tallest in the city.' Building operations began in August 1904, with the demolition of a building to the rear of the Central Hotel and the chairman of the Municipal Council, Mr. F. Anderson, laid the cornerstone of the new building on 21 January 1905. In March 1905 it was announced that the new property would be known as the Palace Hotel. Mr. G. I. Shekury, chairman of the Central Stores Limited, believed 'the Palace will, when completed, we think prove satisfactory in every respect, and your directors are taking a great interest in looking after every detail to make it worthy of its name, and the most perfect hotel in the Orient.' The project, however, was blighted with construction problems from its outset.

A hotel annex, across the road, to the rear of E. D. Sassoon's premises, was secured in 1904 to provide extra accommodation whilst building work was underway. Unfortunately the annex was destroyed by fire in 1907, forcing the company to seek alternative accommodation for its ever-increasing number of would-be guests, many of whom were being turned away. In that year it leased the Metropole Hotel, a mile away on the Bubbling Well Road, opposite the Shanghai Race Course. The hotel, managed by Charlie Biddle, had previously enjoyed notoriety for housing some of Shanghai's most famed foreign prostitutes, so it was little surprise that one of the first things the company did was to change its name to the Grand Hotel.

In March 1906 it was announced that the first block of the Palace Hotel wouldn't be ready for occupation until the coming October, owing to delays caused by

Opposite *A colour rendering of the 'Victorian Renaissance' style Palace Hotel from 1910, displaying the use of colour and architectural detail in its facade*

G. J. Shekury, chairman of the Central Stores, Ltd.

inclement weather. Despite efforts to get the Chinese contractors Wong Fa-kee, who had been recommended by the building's architects Scott & Carter, to hurry things along the hotel didn't open for business until April 1907. At that point the estimated cost of the building had more than doubled to the grand sum of half a million silver dollars.

Upon completion, the old Central Hotel was pulled down and work on building the front part of the hotel on the Bund began in August 1907. Again, building work was slower than expected and two fires, due to faulty flues, alerted the company to the possibility that the structure was dangerous and not up to standard. This fear was compounded when a 20-foot scaffolding pole fell from the top of the building onto the road, narrowly missing a passing foreigner. Despite the surviving 1906 inscription over the main entrance, the building wasn't fully completed until October 1909. However, the fourth and fifth floors were opened on 1 February 1909 in readiness for the landmark meeting of the International Opium Commission. The meeting, attended by representatives from 12 nations, was the first conference to address the world's narcotic's issues, particularly those relating to China, and laid the basis for the first international legislation embodied in the Hague Opium Convention of 1912.

As soon as the hotel was completed, its architects came under intense criticism from Moorhead and Halse, an architectural firm, in a 23-page report, commissioned

Opposite *The newly completed Palace Hotel lobby, 1908*

by the hotel company, detailing their failures in providing proper plans and guidance for the contractors, which introduced 'a gambling element' into the project. The survey was partly prompted by the need to assure future guests that the building was safe, whichever room they might find themselves in. The building was evaluated as something of a 'House that Jack Built,' with the settling process leaving walls, windows and doors askew. Some parts of the building were over eight inches higher in elevation than others and the general finish of the bedrooms was reported to be 'the worst we have yet seen in Shanghai in a building of any pretensions.' The death

B. Bay the Palace Hotel's first manager

Sketch of the roof garden, a popular evening venue, 1911

Opposite *The Palace Hotel dining room, 1908*

THE EZRA ESTATE

Edward I. Ezra, the eldest of four brothers and four sisters born to Isaac Ezra, who established the family trading business in Shanghai in the 1860s, was a larger than life figure and bore considerable civic, social and business responsibilities. Apart from being managing director of The Shanghai Hotels, Limited, he was at the helm of several other businesses, including the Shanghai Gas Company, the Far Eastern Insurance Company, two local newspapers and a large motor garage; alongside being a member of the Shanghai Municipal Council, a Masonic figurehead and vice-president of the Jewish Communal Organisation of China and of the Synagogue.

Educated at the Shanghai Public School, originally a Masonic institution, he passed away just weeks before his 40th birthday. His premature death, as a result of a brain haemorrhage whilst at his office, was sudden and unexpected.

Ezra lived on a massive estate on Avenue Joffre, which a New York correspondent for *The Jewish Tribune* recounted, 'took me a full twenty minutes to traverse. Gardens that make you reminiscent of fairy tales – the open-air swimming pool, the outdoor gymnasium, with electrically operated apparatus; the nine-hole golf course, the beautifully kept hothouses, the several tennis courts, are some of the attractions of only one of many show places in the city owned by the Arabian Jews.'

Reproduced from: Beyond Hospitality: The History of The Hongkong and Shanghai Hotels, Limited.

The fabulously wealthy Edward Ezra in his office, close to the Palace Hotel, 1917

The Grand Hotel on Bubbling Well Road around the time it was leased by Central Stores Limited in 1907

of Mr. Carter during the course of its construction wasn't given any consideration. A substantial out of court settlement by Scott & Carter allowed some wrongs to be put to right and helped eased the company's finances.

Still, the six-storey hotel, with 120 rooms with baths, was the largest and most commodious ever built in China and compared well with the best hotels of Europe and America. The architects placed a strong accent on colour and rendered the building in their locally interpreted 'Victorian Renaissance' design. Most of the ground floor was originally taken over by shops, whilst the top floor accommodated a dining room, which could seat 300 people, as well as a 200-seat banqueting hall with access to a spacious roof garden.

For all its architectural bravura and decorative grandeur, the Palace Hotel's formative years were over-shadowed by an inability to cater for the ever-expanding numbers and fast changing tastes

Devastating fire at the Central Hotel Annex, 1907

of Shanghai society and her visitors. Management problems persisted and there was yet another fire on the roof of the hotel in 1912. Apart from poor management, over-priced facilities and complaints over the quality of the food, the hotel gained a macabre reputation following a series of guest suicides, usually of the bullet through the head variety. For some new arrivals the headache of finding their place in Shanghai society proved too much.

Things began to improve on the hotel front when the fabulously wealthy Edward I. Ezra was elected to the board of Central Stores Limited in 1915. He assumed a major shareholding and, with vision and verve, took the lead in modernising Shanghai's hotel industry. He told shareholders that if they wanted success they 'should be a little more bold, a little more progressive.' His first bold move saw the company purchase the Astor House Hotel, Shanghai's oldest established hostelry, from liquidation in 1915. In keeping with his ambitions the company was re-formed as The Shanghai Hotels, Limited in March 1917. Over the following three years net income at the Palace Hotel had more than doubled and it was yet again turning hordes of would-be guests away.

However, age was catching up with the hotel. Spanish architect Abelardo Lafuente was employed to survey the building, still blighted by inherent structural defects, in 1921. His findings called for the removal of its signature cupolas from the roof (which were rebuilt in a similar fashion in 1998). But the company was soon to face a much more tragic loss as Edward I. Ezra, who had been managing director since January 1920, died on 15 December 1921. His passing left the company's directors with what they described as 'much anxiety' and 'various intricate problems of finance.' Chairman Brodie Clark told the board and shareholders in April 1922, 'as you are all well aware the loss of so important a guiding hand in the administration of the company is one that will make itself felt for a long time to come, and whilst, no doubt, it would have been a comparatively easy matter for Mr. Ezra to adjust, having in mind his enormous financial influence, it is quite another question now that he is no longer with us . . . we are now denied those financial facilities which the late Mr. Ezra's name alone was sufficient to guarantee.'

It wasn't long before The Hongkong Hotel Company, Limited, the colony's oldest established hotel enterprise, dating back to 1865, came to the rescue. Sadly, the company also suffered a great loss in that Sir Ellis Kadoorie, major shareholder and one of the pillars of its board, died of a heart attack in February 1922. Upon his passing, James Harper Taggart, a determined and

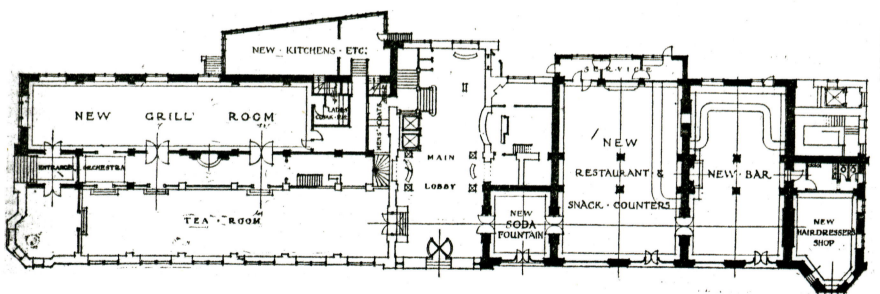

Top *Palace Hotel roof cupola damaged by fire, 1912*

Bottom *Plans for the remodelling of the ground floor of the Palace Hotel, 1926*

dynamic Scotsman and former manager of the Hongkong Hotel, assumed control as managing director of the company. On 12 May 1922 Taggart, at the bequest of the company, acquired Ezra's entire 85 percent holding in The Shanghai Hotels, Limited. In October the following year the two companies were amalgamated and The Hongkong and Shanghai Hotels, Limited was born.

In April 1923 Taggart announced that the Palace Hotel would be rebuilt at some future date. In 1925, with the acquisition of the land on which the hotel stood, which had previously been leased, that date was narrowed down to within the next ten or fifteen years. However, in the meantime, major alterations were proposed for the hotel – not only in the way it looked, but also in the way it worked and played.

Taggart immediately set about 'revolutionising hotel life in quick order,' as one local newspaper later put it. He pioneered the modern hotel business in Shanghai, engineering the creation of new rendezvous and entertainment centres for its social and business circles by injecting new life into the Palace Hotel. Taggart introduced a European-style grillroom, and popularised tea and dinner dances that would become the talk of the town.

The first changes at the hotel were completed in May 1925 when the Palace Hotel Tea Lounge, designed by Abelardo Lafuente and occupying the Nanking Road frontage to the left of the lobby, was opened. Change was soon to come on the management front as well. Mr. Albert E. Willsher, the manager, who had reportedly enhanced the popularity of the hotel tenfold, resigned in September 1926, lured by a lucrative offer from the Grand Hotels,

The new tea lounge and its architect Abelardo Lafuente

Opposite *Architect's impression of the Palace Hotel, 1904*

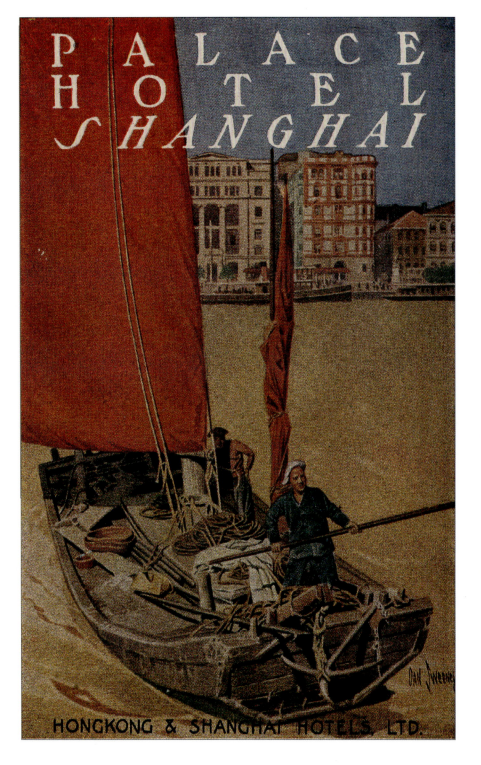

Limited in Calcutta. With him went three heads of department, a seven-piece orchestra and a 'ballet of 16 first-class artists,' reported *The Celestial Empire* newspaper.

Palmer & Turner, architects, drew up further plans for the remodelling in 1926. They involved removing all the shops from the ground floor and introducing an Italian-style grillroom, adjoining the existing tea lounge. Between the two would be an orchestra shell and corridor lined with silk portieres, lit by multi-coloured lights. The plans also included a new soda fountain, adjoining a snack restaurant and a Jacobean-style bar. Modern refrigerated counters and a percolator capable of churning out four gallons of coffee in eight minutes were among the innovations to be introduced. New bronze and glass windows were installed, peaked by a canopy of the same materials extending along the entire Nanking Road frontage. These new facilities opened in April 1927, apart from the grillroom, which opened later in August.

Although the changes dramatically increased the hotel's profitability, the annoying sound of construction on the E. D. Sassoon site opposite the hotel roared to a crescendo in 1929, when the most modern hotel in the Far East opened there. The new Cathay Hotel cast a shadow of doubt over the future of the Palace Hotel and made it even more imperative for the plans for its reconstruction to be realised in a timely fashion.

Top *Stylish hotel brochure cover, designed by American Dan Sweeny*

Opposite *is a view of the Palace Hotel showing south facing balconies, 1914.*

STINK AND PINK AT THE PALACE

Once opened, the Palace Hotel was proud to boast of being the only hotel in the city to feature flush water closets in every guestroom. The hotel was indeed lucky to be equipped with such modern conveniences, as the Shanghai Municipal Council had banned them from public buildings in January 1905. The legislation came too late for it to be enforced at the hotel and attempts to dissuade the company from installing them, stressing concerns about public health, came to nothing.

However, the Council did insist that the sewage from the hotel's large underground tank should be taken away by boat and deposited some distance away on land. Shortly after the hotel opened, an unfamiliar stench emanating from the Whangpoo (Huangpu) River alerted officials to the fact that the boatmen found it much easier just to dump it in the water to save time and effort. In the end, the Council had to resort to the less desirable option of disinfecting the effluent before emptying it into a municipal drain that was discharged – where else? – but into the river right in front of the hotel.

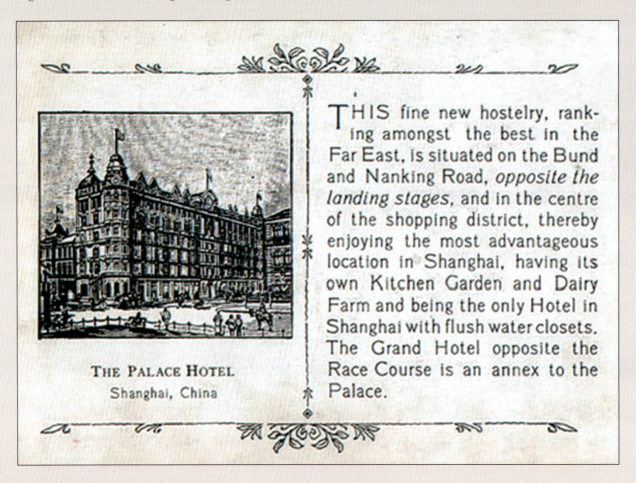

Advert, 1909

Aside from the most hygienic bathrooms in the city, the Palace Hotel also prided itself on the hygienic nature of its food supplies. In anticipation of the hotel's opening, the company purchased a site on Lay Road in the Yangtzepoo (Yangpu) district in early 1906, for conversion into its own kitchen garden and dairy farm. The directors viewed such available products to be 'far from satisfactory' in Shanghai.

Guests were assured that that they could eat the freshest and purest ingredients, grown and cultivated under European supervision. However, one would expect that they wouldn't be too pleased to know that some pigs, imported from Australia in 1911, were 'being fed on hotel refuse, and we hope that in a short time we shall be able to supply hotel guests with wholesome pork and bacon of our own breeding.' With rising property and land values in the district, the site became more of a cash cow over the years, and was sold for a meaty profit in 1917.

Mass catering, the up-to-the-minute kitchen at the Palace Hotel, 1908

3 | THE HOUSE THAT SASSOON BUILT

ELIAS DAVID SASSOON laid the foundation upon which his visionary grandson, Elice Victor Elias Sassoon, was to build a new Shanghai. From its earliest days right up to the 1940's, E. D. Sassoon & Company retained a leading position in the commerce of Shanghai. Over the course of time, banking and financial interests overtook its trading activities, and it was established as a private limited company in 1921. Upon the death of his father in 1924 Victor inherited the title 'Sir,' took over at the helm of the firm, and set about transferring much of the vast family fortune from Bombay to Shanghai. His singular vision was to transform Shanghai into a modern cosmopolitan city with a spectacular new skyline and manners to match.

During a month's stay in Shanghai in May 1928, Sir Victor affirmed his optimism about the future of the city. He remarked to a correspondent of the *North-China Daily News* that although the 'fashion was at present to be parsimonious and to enjoy a quiet evening at home instead of the inevitable champagne parties of six years ago,' there were no signs of a trade depression in Shanghai. Sir Victor listlessly discarded the prevailing pessimism over Shanghai's prospects as a 'largely sentimental pose,' pointing out that land values were higher than on his last visit in 1926. The banks had huge surpluses of funds on hand, which, provided Shanghai remained safe and relatively immune from the troubles in other parts of China, could be used for investment in paying foreign concerns. In Sir Victor's steadfast opinion the inevitable reaction was one towards foreign and Chinese cooperation to the benefit of both in commercial circles.

Sir Victor entered the frame at a most opportune time as building construction in 1929 was forging ahead at unprecedented rates in all parts of the city. Land values were spiralling upwards, making it necessary to build skywards to make returns on investments. Over 22,000 new buildings were constructed in 1929 alone and the value of the site on which Sassoon House

Opposite *The Bund, mid-1920s, with the soon to be demolished offices of E. D. Sassoon to the left*

Portrait of the dashing Sir Victor Sassoon from Fortune *magazine, Jan. 1935*

was built had nearly quadrupled during the course of its construction. A 1930 census put the population of Shanghai at over 2.7 million, around 700,000 more than was popularly estimated, making it the world's sixth largest city.

Sassoon purchased the prominent Arnhold & Co. and its associate, Cathay Land Company, as his vehicle to gain entry to the city. Apart from the Cathay Hotel he also built two huge state-of-the-art hostelries as well as a multitude of apartment blocks, office buildings, theatres, stores and residences around the city. From his office at his headquarters in Sassoon House he saw property values more than treble during the first half of the 1930s. He established E. D. Sassoon Banking Co. Limited, a private banking arm in 1931. Branches of the E. D. Sassoon businesses crossed the continents from Hong Kong, Bombay and Calcutta to Manchester and London. E. D. Sassoon & Co. Limited owned twelve large cotton mills in India and had property holdings in numerous Chinese cities. Such holdings in Shanghai's International Settlement alone were valued at around nine million silver dollars in 1938.

However, the dream was to be short-lived. Sir Victor didn't make Shanghai his personal base until October 1931, and opportunely left the city just ten years later, months before its downfall. He didn't return after the Second World War apart from brief visits in December 1947 and April 1948 to divest some of his business interests. He stood as silent witness as his dreams were perverted and destroyed by the Japanese occupation of the city in 1941, the dissolution of foreign settlements in 1943 and the Communist conquest in 1949. The final downfall caused him to remark that 'I gave up on India and China gave me up.' He married, and passed on his name and his wealth to his Tennessee-born nurse and companion, Evelyn Barnes in 1959. He died, aged 79, in the Bahamas on 12 August 1961. Sir Victor Sassoon left an indelible mark on the character of Shanghai. His name remains familiar and his legacy lives on in the magnificent architecture of the city – most of which survives in timeless style.

Sir Victor was born in Naples in 1881 to Edward Elias Sassoon and Leontine Levy, the stylish daughter of a leading Cairo merchant, whilst they were travelling from England to India. He was educated at Harrow School and Trinity College, Cambridge. With his faintly Eastern appearance, walking stick, natty dress and distinctive moustache he cut a dashing figure – exaggerated by his partial lameness

as a result of a flying accident in the First World War. Sir Victor had a famous passion for horses and built up the largest racing establishment in the Far East. However it is highly unlikely that he made the much reported quip that there was only one greater race than the Jews and that was the Derby! When not at Eves, his rambling Tudor-styled villa in the Shanghai suburbs or at his hotel suite, Sir Victor was most likely to be found in his private box at the Shanghai Race Club or playing golf at the Hungjao (Hongqiao) Club near his home. His love of sports extended into greyhound and motor racing, as well as sailing. He provided the funding for a new Shanghai Yacht Club building in the 1930s.

Sassoon bewildered the Shanghai establishment with his grand plans and ideas, his playfulness and his massive wealth. A 1935 edition of *Fortune* magazine spoke of him in the following terms:

Now Shanghai's No. I realtor, which is a high rank, he lives in the tower of his Cathay Hotel, gives wild, luxurious, and astonishing parties, possesses the only social secretary in the city, strays away to India or England for no more than the few months the British income-tax laws permit him. He is popular in the international set and his immense wealth gives him a special standing. But the crusty diehards of the British colony still look askance at his exuberance and sniff at his ancestry. In England he may hobnob with princes, but in Shanghai, where the Old Guard is almost provincial, there are circles that he cannot enter, partly because he is a Jew, partly because the British deplore his flight from taxation as not quite sporting. He has never married, and if his tastes in women and horses cause comment he can afford to ignore it.

Continuing a long tradition of philanthropy in Shanghai dating back to 1862, when family money paid for the city's first Jewish cemetery, Sir Victor supported numerous humanitarian, medical and educational causes in addition to those concerned with Jewish welfare. Among other accolades his friend Dr. H. H. Kung, the Nationalist Minister of Finance, awarded him the Gold Medal of the First Class for his charitable work with the Red Cross in 1935. The ceremony took place at the Cathay Hotel where he was presented with a large tablet inscribed with the words 'for a virtuous work you give with a willing heart.' Sassoon provided massive support for the thousands of Jewish refugees that flooded into Shanghai from central Europe in the late 1930s. Today, he is remembered in the Bahamas by his widow's endowment of the Sir Victor Sassoon (Bahamas) Heart Foundation.

Copy of a portrait of Sir Victor Sassoon around 1960 which was presented to the Fairmont Peace Hotel in May 2011

ALL ABOUT EVES

Sassoon's former villa, recently in use again as a private residence

Survivng Eves monograms in a glass panel and on the windows of the former Sassoon villa.

Sir Victor Sassoon's hospitality frequently extended far beyond the confines of the Cathay Hotel and into his suburban villa, known as 'Eves' in the Hungjao (Hongqiao) district, bordering his adored golf club. Sassoon biographer, Maisie J. Meyer, remarks that 'hospitality was an art to him and his home was a hub of literary and intellectual life. He enjoyed the society of politicians, artists and writers and encouraged young talent.' Within its ten-acre grounds Sir Victor also 'developed an enthusiasm for gardening and experimented with various species of carnations – he would wear a red one in the morning and white one at night.'

Sir Victor purchased the land for the property from Lt. Col. M. H. Logan, a partner with Palmer & Turner, architects, in late 1932. Within a year Mr. J. W. Williamson, of the same architectural company, had transformed a flat piece of land into one of the most beautiful gardens in Shanghai, featuring small hills, an artificial lake and an old English well. Sassoon's new pied-a-terre, in old English cottage style, was completed within just seven

Top Left *Sir Victor greeting Sir Alexander Cadogan, British Minister to China, at a moonlight party in 1935*

Top Right *Sassoon's former villa, early 1990s*

Bottom: *Eves on the eve of the moonlight party, 1935*

Images of the former Sassoon villa in 2000

months, and was replete with locally crafted furniture and fittings.

The villa, informal in design, was not overly large. Its main feature was a 44-foot by 22-foot living room, or more correctly lounge hall, with a large fireplace and inglenook seats. A staircase to the east of the room reached a gallery, where three bedrooms with attached bathrooms were located. Meyer surmises that Sassoon wished to 'discourage too many people from intruding on his privacy.' One wing contained servants' quarters and garages.

The villa was one in a long line of assets, dating back to his university days, which Sassoon had christened 'Eves' – a contraction of his name, Elice Victor Elias Sassoon. He began his horse racing adventures in India under the name of Mr. Eves, since his father didn't approve of the family name being associated with the sport. He owned horses sporting names such as Dewy Eve, Happy Eve, Holiday Eve, Courting Eve, Wedding Eve, Honeymoon Eve, Opera Eve, among many others, and his stables in England and Ireland bore the same name. Meyer reveals that Sassoon used the nom de plumes Eve Smith and Val Seymour to prevent his parents knowing of his participation in dangerous sports like motor-racing. Of course his cars featured 'Eves' number plates, with EVES 1 being reserved for his Rolls-Royce in Shanghai. Perhaps with some inevitability, he eventually married a woman named Evelyn.

Sir Victor sold Eves to the industrialist, philanthropist, politician and socialite, Mr. James Hsioung Lee in 1946. In more recent times the villa has been used as offices, including those for British Petroleum, and as a private residence.

39

4 ARCHITECTURAL MARVEL

CONSTRUCTION OF THE revolutionary five million silver dollar Sassoon House at No. 20 the Bund began in the spring of 1926. Its architect, George Leopold Wilson, Senior Partner of Palmer & Turner, had originally designed Sassoon House as a 150-foot tall office building and shopping complex containing just 20 luxurious residential apartments. Wilson had already made a significant contribution to the architecture of the Bund before embarking on the design of Sassoon House. His designs included those of the Union Building at No. 4, the Hongkong and Shanghai Banking Corporation at No. 12, the Yokohama Specie Bank at No. 28 and the Glen Line Building at No. 24.

Familiarly known as 'Tug' Wilson, he left London in 1908, at the age of 27, to take up an assistant's position with Palmer & Turner in Hong Kong. Wilson accompanied Lt. Colonel M. H. Logan to Shanghai in 1912 to open a branch office where they both became partners in 1914. He came to Shanghai at a time when the city's prosperity was rising and rapid advances in building technology were being made. Such conditions laid the path for his remarkable influence on the Shanghai skyline.

G. L. Wilson

The latest developments in engineering and construction technology were employed in Sassoon House, which was built on a concrete raft measuring 325 feet by 188 feet, supported by more than 1,600

Opposite *Sassoon House under construction, 1927*

From left to right: F. R. Davey, Lt. Col. M. H. Logan, H. E. Arnhold

piles. The piling system was the first of its kind in Shanghai, with patent Raymond Composite piles made of both concrete and wood, supporting the structure to a depth of 62 feet in the soft mud below.

Construction proceeded as planned, with four floors having been completed by early 1928, when Wilson was informed that he had to stop work on the building as an edict from Sir Victor Sassoon called for the conversion of the upper part of the building into a luxury hotel – a hotel that would bear the name by which Marco Polo knew China – Cathay.

The Cathay Hotels, Limited was formed in Shanghai on 29 May 1928 and incorporated under the Hong Kong Companies ordinances on 7 June 1928. It operated out of premises at nearby 6 Kiukiang (Jiujiang) Road before moving into Sassoon House in 1929. Of the original directors, three were of E. D. Sassoon & Co., namely F. R. Davey, M. J. Moses and F. S. Collett. Other directors included George Leopold Wilson, William R. B. McBain of George McBain, merchants, H. Montague, accountant and H. E. Arnhold. Arnhold & Co. acted as general managers, while Harry Mann acted as

Secretary to the Cathay Hotels, Limited. Prior to Sir Victor's arrival in Shanghai his cousin, Captain Reginald E. Sassoon, represented his company's interests.

Sir Victor Sassoon paid a visit to Shanghai to oversee Wilson's revised plans before giving his final approval for the project to go ahead. The ground floor was altered so as to include a hotel lobby facing Jinkee (Dianchi) Road and a main entrance to Sassoon House and the Cathay Hotel on the Bund. That was the easy part. The hotel called for the addition of two extra floors, considerably increasing the weight of the building and presenting Wilson and his engineers with 'many difficulties.' The extra floors were added after the structural steelwork had been completed by means of reducing the loading from the ground floor upwards. Sassoon House would now only extend upwards to the third floor. Wilson hoped his new design would be 'harmonious,' stating that 'a new note, at least new to Shanghai, was struck.' Wilson viewed

Sassoon House under construction, early and mid-1928

Architect's drawing of the imposing rotunda at the central meeting point of the shopping arcades, December 1925

'good architecture as a creative expression inspired by the beauty of the past and emphasised proportion, mass and form in conjunction with simplicity of interior decoration, colour and lighting in achieving this ideal.' Sassoon House, more than any other structure in Shanghai, epitomised his principles and provided a playground for his imagination.

Shanghai, eager to adopt the fashions and trappings of modern Western living, was quickly catching up with the other great metropolitan cities of the world. As such, the shopping centre planned for Sassoon House was a great novelty, being based on a series of mosaic floored arcades with twenty shops, all under cover. At the intersection of the arcades was a great rotunda, some forty-six feet in diameter, covered with a metal and glass roof. The so-called 'shops-de-luxe' had huge frontages of marble, bronze, plate glass and electro-glazing, all designed to mesmerise Shanghai's fairer sex. Given the ease with which money could exchange hands, two banks, the Banque Belge pour L'Etranger and the Netherlands Trading Society, were conveniently located within the shopping complex. With bronze and glass canopies over the entrances, shoppers could climb into their cars, for which parking was provided on the Bund, without ever coming

THE SPIRIT OF THE CATHAY

Like an Art Deco rocket ship, arising from the impassioned waters of the Whangpoo River, the Cathay Hotel was a powerful symbol of a thrivng Shanghai society. Sleek and elegant, modest in outward adornment, rich and extravagant in its heart, the mood of Shanghai exuded from its walls. It was a multi-layered public place, created with such precision and imagination that all who wandered its corridors or came to rest in its chambers found an intimate friend. The Cathay's personality was indistinguishable from that of its guests.

The Cathay was much more than a social institution. It was the body of Shanghai, an anchor of stability and familiarity, and a Ferris wheel of novelty and surprise. Embodying a vision of the future, it housed the best of the past in a sublime melange of reality and fantasy. The character of the Cathay represented and pandered to every desire of her patrons. Though distinct in physical form, the Cathay was a chameleon being conjured from the minds of a variegated Shanghai society.

The central intersection of the shopping arcades, 1930

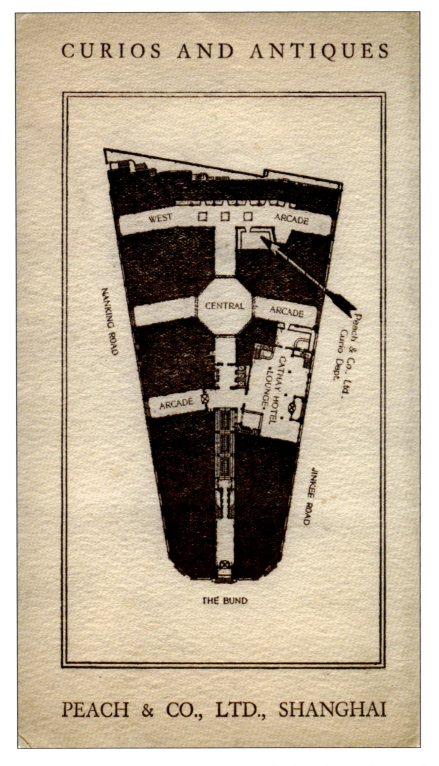

Left *From a Peach & Co. brochure showing the original ground floor plan of Sassoon House*

Right *The Latest Paris fashions, advert, 1929*

into contact with the weather or, indeed, the local population.

Most of the shop units along the Nanking (Nanjing) Road, and in the Sassoon House Arcade were let by May 1928. The owners of Shanghai's most prestigious emporia – high-class dressmakers, milliners, ladies hairdressers and beauty specialists – vied for prime space. Many shops opened some time before the formal opening of Sassoon House. The La Donna Silk Salon Modernique, opened just in time to announce the season's latest hats from Paris. The most fashionable and expensive dress shop in town, owned by Madame Garnet, a White Russian, also found pride of place. Gray's Yellow Lantern Shop offered a charming collection of lingerie, linens, sports clothes and curios for the visiting tourists, including silver swizzle sticks with jade handles and georgette handkerchiefs with lace appliqués. Other units were let to Hirsbunner & Co., the British Flower Shop, Alexander Clarke, Peach & Co., the Bijou Perfumery and to

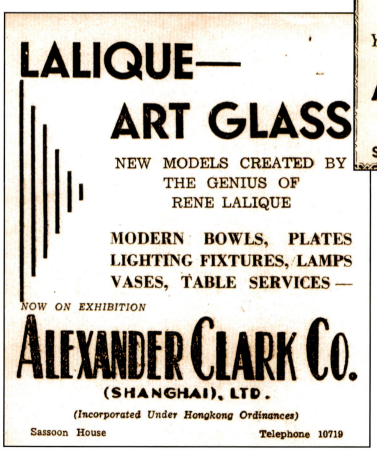

1930s adverts for Alexander Clark in the Sassoon House Arcade

the Municipal Electricity Department for use as a magnificent showroom.

A Bond Street and a Burlington Arcade under one roof. What more could have Shanghai asked for?

The first and second floors were let as offices chiefly to legal firms, doctors, dentists and other professionals. The entire third floor was given over to the offices of Messrs. E. D. Sassoon & Co. Limited, and their associate firm, Arnhold & Co. Limited, with the exception of an extensive group of offices that were let to Messrs. Hanson, solicitors. The front part of the fourth floor was leased to the American Women's Club, as club premises and accommodation. The club, founded in 1898, had around 500 members, comprising roughly half the foreign female population when it took up residence. It had previously held meetings in the Palace Hotel with the aim of allowing 'members and their friends to meet and visit over a cup of tea and choose friends of like interests from among their own country-women and feel at home, at once, in a genuine American companionship, where there is much in common.'

Situated at one of the busiest intersections in Shanghai, the Cathay Hotel provided a peaceful haven from the rush and heat of city life. Its location on the upper floors distanced guests from the hectic street activity below, enabling a wider view of the pastiche that was Shanghai. The calmness and dignity of the Cathay Hotel was reflected in its decor and furnishings. No gaudy colours, no heavy

Right *Municipal Electricity Department's showroom in the Sassoon House Arcade*

Below *1920s advert for Arts & Crafts, Ltd., Asia's foremost interior design company*

mouldings or coarse ornaments, just quiet unobtrusive luxury, marble, bronze, velvet and tapestry.

The hotel was a glorious showplace for the excellence of Shanghai workmanship. The furnishings that were provided by various local firms, including Arts & Crafts, Weeks & Co. and Hall & Holtz, faithfully imitated period styles and created modern designs befitting Shanghai's new cultural entrepôt. Reproductions of old period furniture appeared particularly impressive with cracked, chipped and seared wood blending with stained and faded cane furniture.

Tug Wilson, who practically built the hotel around an arsenal of fashionable Lalique lights, which had caught his attention on a trip home, also moulded much of the interior decor. Lalique was featured everywhere in the hotel, from the public areas to the intimacy of the bathroom where illuminated Lalique shaving mirrors were fitted. Something around 750,000 taels was spent on furnishing and fittings, with over 30,000 taels being spent on Lalique glass alone.

Another 1930s advert for Alexander Clark in the the Sassoon House Arcade

MASTER OF ART
VICTOR STEPANOVICH PODGOURSKY

Caricature of Victor Podgoursky by his friend, the renowned Russian cartoonist Sapajou, 1935

Shanghai's substance and mood – its modernism and its place as Asia's principal industrial and commercial hub, was represented in allegory and art throughout the Cathay Hotel; art in the finest form, stemming from the imagination of famed resident Russian artist Victor Stepanovich Podgoursky.

Podgoursky arrived in Shanghai on board a small Chinese ship soon after graduating from the Moscow School of Painting, Sculpture and Architecture, in 1918. Victor, who was the eldest of four children, was accompanied by brother Eugene on the journey. Podgoursky worked as a political caricaturist for the newspaper *Shanghai Life*, and went on to teach at the Shanghai Academy of Arts and become a leading light at the Shanghai Art Club. Before turning his eye to the Cathay Hotel he had completed stunning murals and sculptures in many prominent Shanghai buildings including the French Club, the Palace Hotel and the Capitol Cinema.

His imposing, colourful murals of industry and mystical cities hung above the subtle marble walls on the ground floor of Sassoon House and the Cathay Hotel, where his work extended upwards in the form of striking stained-glass compositions, grille-work and decorative relief, including the famous greyhound insignia featured in and outside the hotel, and on its literature and postcards.

Following his return to the USSR with his wife and their 26-year old son, Valery, in 1947, Podgoursky taught drawing, art, design, anatomy and sculpture at Kazan Art College. However, it was not a happy homecoming as a series of tragic events, commencing with Mrs. Podgoursky's bereavement after the imprisonment of Valery, befell the family. Later Eugene committed suicide and younger brother Konstantin, chief of the Red Guards, was martyred by White Czechs. Surviving sibling Sonya died in Moscow while engaged in political activities for the youth wing of the Communist party. Victor Stepanovich Podgoursky died in Tashkent in 1969.

50

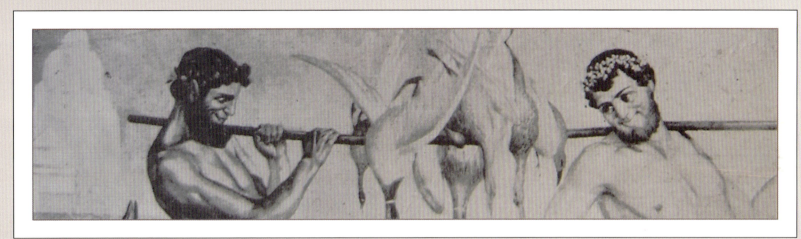

Some of Podgoursky's magnificent mural panels that once decorated the walls of the Cathay Hotel

5 | A NEW ERA FOR SHANGHAI

THE CATHAY HOTEL formally opened on 1 August 1929. Numerous critics and sceptics had foretold of its failure, arguing that Shanghai already had far too many hotel rooms. Others suggested that it was too large, too lavish and too expensive. They were all proved wrong as the hotel lived up to its soubriquet as the 'Claridges of the Far East.' The opening of the Cathay heralded a new era for Shanghai and indeed for hotels throughout the Far East – a pacesetter brimming with the latest amenities and luxuries, and a monument to the marriage of art and technology. Whilst the advent of the Cathay Hotel cast a shadow of antiquity over the neighbouring Palace Hotel, it ignited a dazzling beam of optimism over Shanghai's future in that Sir Victor Sassoon had so wholeheartedly committed himself to such a grandiose and futuristic venture.

Mr. E. Carrard, the hotel's Swiss manager, invited a large group of important officials, businessmen and journalists for dinner and an inspection tour of the hotel on the evening before the opening. Three of the four floors of guest rooms had already been completed. The press lauded the dinner as one of the most sumptuous ever served in Shanghai and printed mouth-watering accounts of the hotel's grandeur. Journalist Edna Lee Booker, reported that the hotel opened in a blaze of sophisticated splendour – 'in our party were a number of Chinese girls. We of the European world wore trailing French creations which bared our backs. But the women of the Orient wore clinging, seductive gowns which were made high in the neck and long in the sleeve, but whose scant skirts were cut with tantalizing slits up either side.'

An after dinner speech by Mr. H. E. Arnhold, Chairman of the Shanghai Municipal Council and a director of the hotel company, emphasised the role of the Cathay Hotel in fulfilling a long felt need

E. Carrard, the Cathay Hotel's first manager

Opposite *Shanghai's new icon of modernity stands tall on the Bund, 1930*

Top-flight entertainment and dancing, 1931 advert

of the central district for a first-class hostelry that catered for high-spending casual visitors rather than permanent residents. Following the repast the Cathay Hotel Dance Orchestra, under the direction of Henry Nathan from New York, wooed the crowd into the wee hours.

Sassoon had persuaded Carrard to give up his position as manager of the famed Taj Mahal Hotel in Bombay and follow him to Shanghai. Sassoon's right-hand man from India, Commander F. R. Davey, formerly head of E. D. Sassoon & Co. in Calcutta, followed too. Davey was described by *Fortune* magazine as 'the picture of an English Squire,' hard-headed, energetic and reserved, whose relationship with Sir Victor was based not upon similarities, but on opposites.

Carrard had formerly managed some of the best hotels in London, Paris and Rome. Sponsored by *The China Press*, a local newspaper, the first guest to inscribe her name in the Cathay Hotel register was Mrs. 'Buddy' Hazel, a budding playwright from New Jersey. On her way home from Manila she described the Cathay Hotel as truly one of the most elaborate and up-to-date hotels to be found anywhere in the world. Celebrated American columnist Karl Kitchen agreed, reporting that it boasted 'many features that surpasses anything

I have seen at home or abroad, likewise there is no hotel in the world which offers such a wide variety of appointment – but if you live in New York you will have to travel nearly 8,000 miles to see it!'

Most resident or casual visitors would have entered the hotel and its ground floor lobby lounge, either through its direct entrance on Jinkee (Dianchi) Road, or through one of the shopping arcade entrances in Sassoon House. The principal and most imposing entrance was from the Bund, where, on entering, guests would be instantly exposed to the gallant splendour of the hotel. The entrance hall, with its marble walls and coffered coved ceiling, decked out in rich colours, faced a black marble staircase with a heavy bronze balustrade. On the first landing three stained-glass windows depicting industry and commerce, agriculture and the meeting of East and West, shone in the faces of those ascending to the sanctity of their offices above. On either side of the staircase two express lifts vaulted visitors directly to the public areas on the upper floors of the hotel.

Passing under the stairs, the inner corridor lounge was subtly lit through magnificent stained glass ceiling panels. Above its marble-clad walls, colourful murals depicting the industries of all nations

Ultra-stylish opening advert featuring a drawing of the Tower Grill on the ninth floor, 1929

Shanghai's commercial ambitions in this stained glass window greeted those with offices in Sassoon House

unfolded along the corridor. With tables nestled amongst palms the corridor was not just a passage, but also a sophisticated spot to sip cocktails and entertain friends.

Moving into the neighbouring lobby lounge, light grey and rose mottled marble panels edged by dove grey marble strips gave it an air of dignity usually associated with the very best of European and American hotels. Murals of imaginary cities in various architectural styles, painted in soft colours, enveloped its interior. Accents of colour from the marble floors, the ceiling and the royal blue velvet curtains were adopted in the soft furnishings. Two large balconies on the east and west sides of the lobby separated the sexes and their intimate conversations on relevant topics of the day. The western balcony was reserved for gentlemen, with a barbers shop and the hotel manager's office behind, whilst the opposing side was reserved for ladies. A small balcony over the lobby clock was set aside for performances from one of the Cathay Hotel's three resident orchestras. Joseph Ullstein's Concert Orchestra performed classical selections daily to accompany the Thé Dansant and the Dinner Dansant. The adjoining Cathay Bar, with its Gothic Tudor interior of stone and rusticated wood presented a mannish parody to the lobby's sensual and subtle

Top left *The lobby, 1930*

Bottom left *Cathay Hotel reception, 1930*

Top right *Bund entrance lobby, 1930*

Middle right *The new hotel bar, 1933*

Bottom right *The remodeled lobby lounge, 1933*

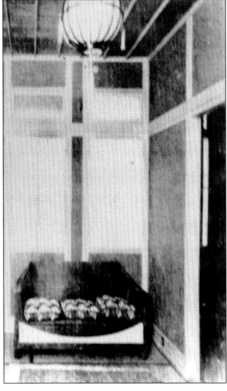

Cathay Hotel Suites in different designs, including Japanese, Indian, Futuristic, Jacobean, and Chinese.

mood. Part of the lobby had been remodelled in late 1933 for this new addition to the hotel's store of entertainment venues.

The intricate attention given to the decor and colour scheme did not halt at the ground floor. Each floor containing hotel rooms was modelled separately with regards to its colour scheme, carpets, curtains and bed covers. Buff brown and green carpets layered the softly lit, stone-clad corridors punctuated by handsome walnut doors.

The fourth to seventh floors housed 214 hotel rooms and suites. The hotel also boasted nine 'apartements de-luxe,' each with a bedroom, sitting room, dining room and two bathrooms. Their vast marble bathtubs came with silver taps and purified water pumped from the Bubbling Well Spring, over two miles from the hotel. The 'apartements' were of uncompromising luxury and embodied a variety of national and historical styles. There were two old English suites, one in Jacobean and one in Georgian style. The former had oak panelled walls, stone and brick fireplaces and model plaster ceilings. The Georgian suite, with panelled walls finished in cream, featured a handsome brass hob grate. The Indian suite with filigree plasterwork on

> CATHAY HOTEL
> Shanghai
> Cablegrams: "Cathotel"
>
> 215 ROOMS AND SUITES
> each with private Bathroom
>
> Single and Double Room Rates, which are inclusive, according to location and size of accommodation required
>
> Monthly terms, by arrangement
>
> SUITES—
> in various attractive furnishings:
>
> Modern English   Modern French
> Jacobean   Futuristic
> Indian   Chinese
> Japanese   Georgian
>
> E. CARRARD,
> Manager.

Top *An opportunity to tour the world in one hotel, early 1930s advert*

Bottom *Chinese style Cathay Hotel suite*

Sassoon House stands tall in the heart of the International Settlement, 1930

the walls and ceilings was littered with richly coloured Indian carpets. Reputable Chinese and Japanese craftsmen were employed to ensure that the suites accredited to their respective countries were resplendent to the finest detail. A moon gate separated the sitting room and dining room of the Chinese suite. An Imperial dragon design on the ruddy red ceiling complemented its red lacquer furniture offset by gold walls.

The Japanese suite was a replica of a Japanese house with the exception that no 'ta-tamis', or floor mats, were to be found. The sitting room and dining room were of natural wood with plaster panels, some treated with gold leaf. Its particularly attractive bedroom had gold walls and a natural wooden painted ceiling with black lacquer ribs. Two modern French suites, as well a modern English suite, exemplified styles currently fashionable in Europe and America, whilst an ultra-modern suite paraded a lifestyle of the future.

The eighth floor was devoted to dining and dancing. Emerging from the lift, visitors passed through a landing speckled with Lalique glass into an upper lounge that overlooked Nanking Road and the river. Inside, Lalique figures set in niches and wall plaques in opalescent glass softly illuminated the dull silver and gold room. The lounge opened on one side to the Peking Room and to the dining and ballroom on the other.

The Peking Room was created in 1933 from the fabric of a modern-style reading and writing room that was lined with bird's-eye maple and teak, and illuminated by Lalique ceiling fittings composed of many sections held together by silver rings. Its conversion into an architectural extravaganza in purely Chinese style was partly prompted by the desires of wealthy American tourists. It was the place to go for tiffin (an adopted Indian term for a light meal or lunch) and contained all the treasures that visitors expected to see in China in one room, replete with the all-important modern luxury of air-conditioning. Carrard

worked closely with Palmer & Turner, and Peach & Co. in modelling the new grillroom. Their object was to 'create an attraction based upon a harmonious, but unusual, design with unsurpassed excellence in cuisine and service. Motifs from Peking's temples were adopted in an effort to create an attraction that was 'pure and true to Chinese tradition.'

The dragon assumed a central position in the design of the restaurant's ceiling panels. Being the chief figure of Chinese mythology, with the ability to control the rains (symbolising peace and prosperity) and the power to rise from earth to heaven, the dragon came to represent the Emperor. The Empress was symbolised in the design through the figure of a phoenix. These figures, surrounded by rain clouds, were arranged around a flaming pearl – a symbol of perfection. Towards the outer edge of the rain clouds, a bat entered the design, typifying happiness and luck. The ceiling panels were adopted from door panels of the Hall of Blending the Great Creative Forces in Peking's Forbidden City.

The beams and metal grille-work were decorated with the conventionalised lotus – daughter of the rains and the sacred flower of Buddhism – a symbol of Buddhist paradise. Features on the beams were also taken from the Forbidden City, namely the Palace of Heavenly Purity and the Gate of Supreme Harmony, as well as from the Temple of Heaven. The motif found on the columns was taken from a western gallery in the Forbidden City.

The latticed grilles over the windows incorporated characters of long life and

Top *The eighth-floor reading and writing room before its conversion to the Peking Room in 1933*

Bottom *Part of the Peking Room and adjoining lounge following its completion in 1933*

61

"THE CATHAY"—the most modern Hotel in China, has : 214 Rooms and Suites each with private bathroom. 9 Three-roomed "Apartements de Luxe," each comprising bedroom with two bathrooms, sitting-room and dining-room. Dining-room and Ball-room (with sprung white maple floor) and Lounges on Eighth Floor opening on to spacious roof-gardens and terraces, with magnificent river views. Modern ventilating system providing purified heated or cooled air, according to season, in all public rooms. Cuisine by well-known French chef and three French assistant chefs. Service under supervision of experienced European *Maîtres d'Hôtel*. All visible light fittings in public rooms by Lalique. Separate concert and dance orchestras.

Cable :—" CATHOTEL, SHANGHAI."

E. CARRARD, *Manager*.

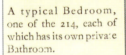

A typical Bedroom, one of the 214, each of which has its own private Bathroom.

The Dining-room and Ball-room on Eighth Floor, opening to the South on to spacious terraces.

Staying in the lap of luxury, a section from an early 1930s hotel brochure

happiness in their many conventionalised forms, and were adapted from a grille in the Yi-Yuen Hall, again in the Forbidden City. The air-duct grilles were based on the characters for longevity and the 'endless knot' – one of the eight Buddhist emblems of happy augury. All of the decorative plaster and metal work was executed by one of Shanghai's most famous sculptors, Mr. W. W. Wagstaff. His son's paintings of a Yangtsze village, the Great Wall and Hong Kong also adorned the west wall of the room.

A vista of the magnificent main dining and ballroom was afforded from the upper lounge through a pair of oxidised silver gates. It could also be approached through an anteroom that formed a second lounge. Rose tinted curtains and carpets splashed with gold, dull

Eighth-floor lounge, early 1930s

silver and gold walls, white birch furniture, a white maple dance floor and, of course, a liberal show of Lalique lighting fused together, creating one of the most beautiful dining rooms in the world. From the Lalique studio, ten individually sculpted draped female figures in glass, the Ladies of the Fountain – set in niches and illuminated, numerous ceiling lights, sparrow wall plaques and half-bowls – graced the lofty hall.

The main illumination of the ballroom was by indirect lighting with special dimmers used to regulate subtle colour changes through rose-tinted glass fanlight panels – one colour melting into another, producing an effect of sunrise and sunset, blazing daylight and moonlight. Other lighting was concealed in the cornices and pyramidal glass lanterns mounted in the ceiling. The southerly facing dining room opened on to three terraces covered with awnings. To accommodate even more guests in even greater comfort, the dance floor was moved to the middle of the room and given a new ovular shape, and a terrace facing Nanking (Nanjing) Road was opened containing a small cocktail bar in 1931. The ballroom was redecorated and further remodelled in 1935.

Ascending to the ninth floor, visitors were transported to another fairy-tale palace in a Chinese style. On the wall of the staircase landing a large Chinese landscape painting was brushed with light from butterfly-patterned lights of Korean design and an illuminated Lalique golden carp. Up ahead, two blackwood doors, each set with circular Lalique glass panels with gold fish

The exquisitely designed Tower Grill, 1933

designs opened onto the Chinese-styled Tower Grill. The restaurant was richly decorated in green and gold relieved by black and red lacquer, with gilded panels of Chinese carving set in the pilasters and piers. Chinese temple artists painted the restaurant's coffered ceiling, incorporating symbols of good augury and good luck. Antique bronze Buddhas and yet another Lalique illuminated golden carp crowned the hoard of treasures. Bold inscriptions in Chinese characters appeared on three vermilion boards:

The Tower Grill, 1930

The hall is filled with honourable guests
As the fish loves water so love I pleasure
Fine wines from the four seasons.

The grillroom was converted into the Tower Night Club, Shanghai's most chic and fashionable nightspot, which opened on 19 October 1935.

Climbing again, the upper floors of the Cathay Hotel tower were of a demonstratively English character, taking visitors back to the best period of English medieval architecture. The tenth-floor Jacobean style banqueting hall, with its modelled ceiling, carved panelling and mammoth mantelpiece, was a tribute to the craftsmanship of Shanghai firms. The eleventh floor above was originally a series of private dining rooms, but, following Sassoon's 1931 full-time move to Shanghai, it was there that he kept his personal suite. The balcony on the tower at the apex of the hotel was for the exclusive use of the Shanghai Fire Brigade as a lookout. Almost uninterrupted views across Shanghai's smoky haze could be seized at an elevation ten feet higher than the tower at the Custom House further along the Bund. A white light at the pinnacle of the tower signified all was well, while a red one alerted danger.

Opposite *Something to write home about, early 1930s postcard*

"THE CATHAY"—the most modern Hotel in China

Cable:—"CATHOTEL, SHANGHAI."

6 | THE CATHAY SISTERS

Sir Victor Sassoon did little by halves. By the time that the Cathay Hotel had opened its doors work on another one of his luxury hotels, the Cathay Mansions, was nearing completion and work on yet another, the Metropole, would soon start. Yet again, 'Tug' Wilson of Palmer & Turner, Architects was entrusted with their design.

Times were moving fast and, just as with the change of plan for Sassoon House to be partly converted into a hotel, the site where the Metropole Hotel was built was originally earmarked for another Sassoon office and residential property to be known as Hamilton House. It was anticipated that the building would be completed by 1 January 1931. However, work began on building the Metropole Hotel on that site in October 1929 and in the following month Sassoon finally secured an adjacent plot for the construction of Hamilton House. Both buildings, towering 14-storeys high, were to be built in a complementary Gothic Art Deco style partly determined by Shanghai Municipal Council building regulations, requiring the upper floors to be stepped back and tapered. The buildings were also set back from the intersection of today's Fuzhou and Jiangxi Roads allowing the realisation of the Shanghai Municipal Council's long cherished scheme to form of a central circus in the heart of the International Settlement. The Council's offices, opposite the Metropole Hotel, opened in 1922, were designed with such in mind. Another building that would enclose the circle, that of the Metropolitan Land Company, was also planned in 1929. However this wasn't achieved until 1936, when the Commercial Bank of China building was completed on the remaining site.

The circus, dubbed by *The Shanghai Times* newspaper as Shanghai's 'Piccadilly Circus,' was never a roundabout, as some believe. All four buildings still survive today, on what remains one of Shanghai's most awe-inspiring downtown locations.

The pace of construction for the Metropole Hotel broke all records with its

Opposite *Magazine advert for the 'Cathay Sisters', 1933*

entire 14-storey structure having been built in just three months in 1930. However, its completion was delayed by a general labour strike in late 1931 and the Sino-Japanese conflict around Shanghai in early 1932. When opened on 1 March 1932, the 200-room Metropole was the fourth-largest hotel in the International Settlement, and as to be expected it was luxuriously appointed. 'Tug' Wilson used simplicity as the keynote of design, with Jacobean furniture and Persian rugs being placed in the bedrooms and the public areas.

The Metropole was primarily designed to meet the needs of commercial visitors, rather than tourists, as well as those of local residents. The dark panelled walls of its 300-seat banquet room were more inclined to host business meetings and gatherings than scenes of folly. The Rotary Club of Shanghai, which was founded in 1919, held their weekly Thursday lunchtime meetings there. Sassoon hosted their first function on 17 March 1932 and spoke to the 125 assembled Rotarians on the commercial and trade links between East and West.

Architect's rendition of the futuristic Sassoon twin towers, with the Metropole Hotel to the left and Hamilton House to the right

The ornate ground floor lobby, grill room and banquet room at the Metropole Hotel, early 1930s

He 'emphasised the fact that the West will never be able to keep furnishing the Orient with industrial manufactures if it does not also provide some means to increase the buying power of the peoples the machine-made goods are intended for.' How the tables have turned today! However the room also played host to some of Sir Victor Sassoon's whimsical parties. On one occasion in 1934 he invited over sixty children from 'local society' to come along dressed as animals from Noah's Ark. Venerably attired as Noah, Sassoon may have been disappointed, but more likely amused, that the most popular form of dress amongst his young guests was not at all from biblical times, but of a 1928 vintage – the same year that he acquired the hotel site – Mickey Mouse!

Essentially the Metropole was a gentlemen's hotel that presented itself in the same manner as her prosperous business guests, who would be accustomed to hobnobbing with statesman and captains of industry. Its grillroom was a popular venue for businessmen and groups of pals to get together over a flagon of UB (United Brewery)

Locally produced United Brewery (UB) beer was on offer at all Cathay Hotels, Limited properties

Top *The Metropole Hotel reception, 1933*

Bottom *Lightning pace construction - the Metropole Hotel in August (left) and December 1930 (right)*

beer accompanied by steak and chips. The room resembled an old English inn with exposed brick, dark wood panelling, driftwood furniture and an enormous fireplace. Visiting captains of industry would stay in one of the voluminous suites on the upper floors that opened onto private roof gardens with panoramic views of the city.

The Metropole Hotel also occupied the sixth floor of Hamilton House after the latter opened in October 1932. It featured two-room suites and single rooms with room-service at breakfast times. Hamilton House was largely a residential building, though its light and airy offices on the first to third floors were occupied by commercial enterprises including banks and

shipping offices. All other floors contained high-class apartments, replete with fully equipped kitchens and pantries including refrigerators and electric stoves. An extension to Hamilton House, running east on Foochow (Fuzhou) Road, was started in May 1931 and completed just over two years later, allowing space for more offices and apartments. The most luxurious triplex apartments in the city were housed in Hamilton House, and numerous medical and dental practitioners, who combined their offices or residential suites with surgeries, were to be found in the building.

The sculpted granular and angular faces of the Metropole Hotel and Hamilton

Views of the main dining room at the Metropole Hotel above and to the right

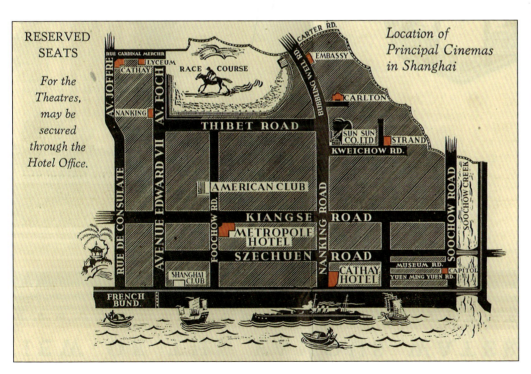

Opposite *In the heart of cinema land, from a 1932 brochure*

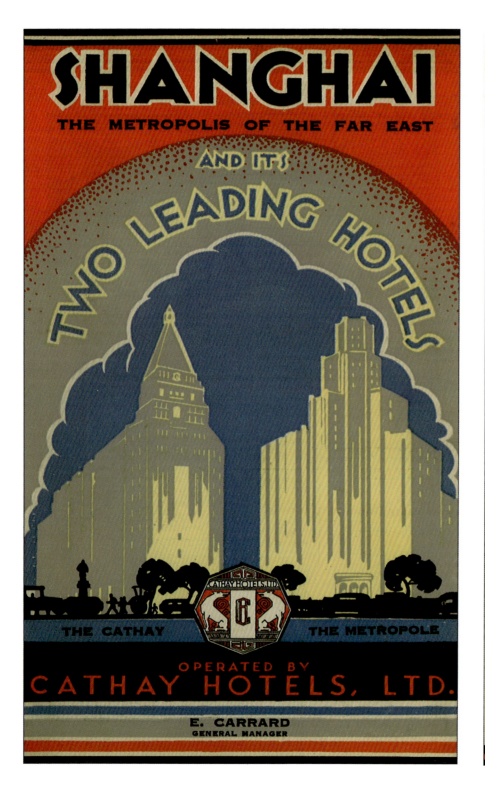

The CATHAY

Cable Address: "CATHOTEL"
ROBERT TELFER, Manager

The Most Luxuriously Appointed Hotel in the FAR EAST . . . .

Situated at the corner of Nanking Road and the Bund, commanding an unsurpassed view of the River and City.

Nine Three-roomed *Apartements de Luxe*, each comprising bed-room with two bath-rooms, sitting-room and dining-room.

Dining-room and Ball-room (with sprung white maple floor), and Lounges on Eighth floor opening on to spacious roof-gardens and terraces, with magnificent river views.

Modern ventilating system, providing purified heated or cooled air, according to season, in all public rooms. Cuisine by well-known French chef and three French assistants.

250 ROOMS and SUITES

Each with Private Bath

RATES (*American Plan*)

Single Room with Bath
From Mex. $20.00 per day
Double Room with Bath
From Mex. $35.00 per day

SUITES
Single, Mex. $35; Double Mex. $50 upwards

(Rates vary according to size and location of rooms.)

The METROPOLE

Cable Address: "METHOTEL"
EDWARD O. ARREGGER, *Manager*

Shanghai's newest and most modern Commercial and Residential Hotel . .

Situated at the corner of Foochow and Kiangse Roads, in the heart of the Banking, Shopping, and Commercial Centres.

Many rooms have their own private balconies from which unsurpassed views of the City and River may be obtained.

Spacious Lounges, Dining and Grill Room, American Bar, and Banquet Room, with seating capacity for approximately 300 Persons.

200 ROOMS

Each with Private Bath

RATES (*American Plan*)

Single Room with Bath
       From Mex.$15.00 per day

Double Room with Bath
       From Mex.$25.00 per day

Monthly rates upon application to the Manager

fully centrally heated and air-cooled, and under the sole management of Mr. Edward Arreggor. Arreggor, who had managed hotels in London, the south of France and Egypt, arrived in Shanghai in January 1932, fresh from three years in Hong Kong.

Whilst the Metropole Hotel's appearance resembled that of a New York skyscraper, the Cathay Mansions wore a very British face, even though it was located far away from the British dominated commercial heart of the city in an upcoming, stylish district of the French Concession.

House were finished in Suzhou granite on the first floor and with a special artificial stone finish above. Sassoon set up his own construction business, the Aerocrete Company, under the chairmanship of Commander F. R. Davey, to produce a new lightweight building material for their internal walls and partitions. Both buildings were

Cathay Mansions under construction in December 1928 and following completion in 1929

Opposite *Cathay Hotels, Limited luggage label*

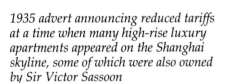

1935 advert announcing reduced tariffs at a time when many high-rise luxury apartments appeared on the Shanghai skyline, some of which were also owned by Sir Victor Sassoon

Designed as a luxurious residential hotel for visitors as well as long-term residents, Cathay Mansions, the largest building in Asia, formally opened in December 1929. It stood across the road from the magnificent Cércle Sportif Française, the French Club, boasting 17 tennis courts on its lawn, which had been completed in 1926.

The Gothic inspired 14-storey hotel featured 279 single rooms that could be configured to form two, three or four room suites. The principal entrance from Rue Bourgeat (Changle Road) opened onto a spacious tea lounge, with four high-speed Otis lifts behind. The ground floor also featured a sun lounge and an arcade with five luxury shops leading to a secondary entrance opposite the French Club. Shops were also found alongside the north and west sides of the building.

Above the ten floors of hotel rooms, a main dining room finished in teak and oak, and capable of seating 250 was located on the eleventh floor. A large lounge, two private dining rooms, a bar and two card rooms were also found there. Sixteen exclusive private apartments were laid out on the twelfth floor, whilst above accommodation for well over 100 Chinese servants was provided for. Atop was a commanding roof garden, 170-feet above ground level. Shanghai's largest skyscraper was luxuriously furnished by a number of local firms, including Arts & Crafts and Sing Tai. Prices for the suites were graded according to elevation and to furnishings, with the higher floors naturally being the most expensive.

Special attention was paid to the needs of children, with carefully laid out gardens and a play area in front of the hotel. The young folk also had their own dining room, hand-painted in pastels with flowers and animals, and furnished with pigeon-egg blue tables and chairs coming in an assortment of sizes to please all ages. During less playful times in 1932, when Sino-Japanese hostilities were raging, large numbers of senior foreign military personnel made the hotel their home.

In late 1931, just before the hostilities started, Sassoon announced that he was to build an apartment building called Grosvenor House to accompany Cathay Mansions on what would be known as the Cathay Estate. His ambition to have it ready for occupation by spring 1933 was, unfortunately, thwarted by the tyranny of the times. When it eventually opened in mid-1935, the monolithic Art Deco 17-storey building lived up to its billing as the most modern and luxurious in the city. Again designed by Tug Wilson of Palmer & Turner, there were apartments of every

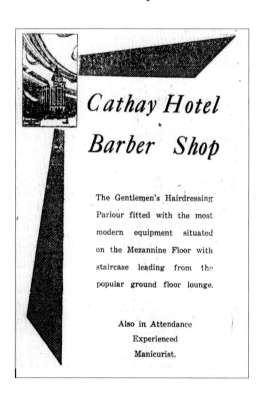

Top *A familiar business rendezvous, advert for the American Bar at the Metropole Hotel, 1936*

Left *The Cathay Hotel also offered services for the discerning gentleman*

The resplendent Majestic Hotel building

size and tenants could choose whether they wanted one decorated in Old English or American Colonial style. The neighbouring Cathay Flats and shops facing Moulmein (South Maoming) Road were also completed around the same time, though a plan to build another huge building on the estate never materialised.

More of an adopted orphan than a Cathay sister, the Cathay Hotels, Limited took over the operation of the Majestic Hotel in April 1930. Whilst the Cathay sisters flaunted mass and modernity, the petite Majestic boasted elegance and sophistication crafted from an earlier period of Shanghai's history. Its palatial main building, formerly known as Cecile Court, was erected as a home for the McBain family. Patriarch George McBain, who had made his fortune in shipping and oil, unfortunately did not live to see its completion in 1906. It was converted into the Majestic Hotel under the ownership of The Hongkong and Shanghai Hotels, Limited and opened in November 1924.

In appearance and manner the Majestic was much more than a hotel – it was a country-like estate unrivalled in terms of grandeur, luxury and dignity. Its beautifully laid out ten-acre grounds featured an old English garden, as well as one of the finest Italian gardens in the Far East.

Under the supervision of Spanish architect Abelardo Lafuente the mansion was renovated inside and out, though its characteristic features and contents, including a wealth of old paintings, priceless tapestries and imposing marble settings, were retained. On entering visitors would pass

1933 plans for the Cathay Estate with the Cathay Mansions and Grosvenor House to the right. The central tower was never built.

though an Italian marble vestibule into an oak-panelled hall opening onto the classically-styled dining room, a Chinese-style smoking room lined with priceless blackwood made from chests looted from the Forbidden City in Beijing during the Boxer Rebellion in 1901, a library in French Gothic style, a billiard room, and the hotel's main lounge and drawing room. The lofty oak-panelled lounge featured a ten-foot high Sienna marble mantelpiece as its centrepiece. The Louis XVI drawing room was decorated with groups of marble statues and precious objets d'art, as well as an Erard grand piano purchased by Mrs. McBain at a cost of £2,000. The ground floor also housed the Empire Banqueting Room, replete with a bronze bust of Napoleon.

The hotel's individually crafted suites were the last word in luxury. The Embassy Suite, its finest, featured a Boucher painted ceiling of flower-laden cupids amongst rose-tinted clouds. Royalty, film stars and multi-millionaires made it their home when visiting the city. Foreign ministers, Chinese provincial governors and Maharajahs came and went.

As part of the hotel conversion an additional wing was built accommodating a magnificent winter garden and a ballroom of unrivalled splendour. Its dance floor, 100-feet across, was laid out in the shape of a four-leaf clover with a marble and bronze fountain with a mermaid arising from the waters as its central feature. The ballroom at the Majestic Hotel was reputed to be the best in the Far East, if not the entire planet, and was the setting for the marriage of Generalissimo Chiang Kai-shek and Soong May-ling in December 1927.

Top *The Embassy Suite was the finest, featuring a ceiling painted with flower-laden cupids.*

Bottom *The richly decorated and furnished drawing room*

Top Left *Advert from June 1930 offering the possibility of a pleasant evening before the full onslaught of the hot, sultry Shanghai summer*

Top Right *A Russian jazz band playing in the Majestic Ballroom*

Bottom *The Majestic Hotel Ballroom, a fine building in a fine setting*

The right clientele, sketch from a 1930 advert for the Majestic hotel, 'Shanghai's most popular rendezvous'

Shanghai society was stunned by the unexpected news, announced in a local newspaper in December 1929, that the hotel was to be sold to a Chinese real estate company. Yet, soon after that sale the property was transferred into the hands of the Shanghai Land Investment Company, in which Sir Victor Sassoon had a large stake, and the hotel and its ballroom continued to operate as normal. The legendary Whitey Smith Orchestra continued to syncopate and Shanghai's most famous dancing duo, Joe and Nellie Farren, continued to scintillate. Even Mr. Robert Telfer, who had managed the hotel since it opened, continued in his post, having switched his allegiance to the Cathay Hotels, Limited. However, the engagement was short-lived as the hotel rooms were quietly closed down and their contents auctioned off in September 1930. H. G. Woodhead, editor of the *North-China Daily News*, no doubt with Sir Victor Sassoon and the Cathay Hotel in mind, believed that 'there will never be another hotel in Shanghai so replete with charm, no matter how thoroughly modern, comfortable, luxurious, electricized, and Americanized, the new buildings may be.'

The ballroom remained open until the end of March 1931. On the occasion of the last dinner dance, the *North-China Daily News* reported that 'the closing of the

Majestic Ball Room...
SHANGHAI

Cathay Hotels, Ltd., on behalf of the Shanghai Land Investment Company, beg to announce that The Majestic Ball Room will close after:

SUNDAY, MARCH 29th, 1931

Until that date the Ball-Room will remain open EVERY evening, with the exception of Sunday evenings' for "DINNER-DANSANT" with:

MR. SERGE ERMOLL'S
Popular Dance Orchestra
and added

ENTERTAINMENT PROGRAMME

Featuring

MISS NINA ANTERES
(Original Repertoire)

MR. BOLSHAKOFF-DIMOFF
(Balalaika Virtuoso)

Patrons of the Majestic are assured that, during the period the Ball-Room will remain open, the present standard of Catering, Wines, Music, and Entertainment will be fully maintained.

SUNDAY AFTERNOON TEA DANCE
will be held every Sunday between 5 and 8 p.m., with:

COMBINED CATHAY and MAJESTIC JAZZ SYMPHONY
Under direction of

MR. HENRY NATHAN

Reservations Phone 34231

THE CATHAY HOTELS, LTD.
E. CARRARD.—General Manager.

Majestic Hotel was a sentimental reason for considerable revelry in its ballroom on Saturday night. So anxious was Shanghai to say its farewells in the proper fashion that by 9.30 people were being turned away at the front door while 738 diners were trying to find elbowroom inside. Champagne flowed like water and the party soon assumed the proportions of one of the national balls. At midnight there were 1,100 dancers on the floor trying to make the best of the precious few hours left.'

Sir Victor Sassoon was yet again part of a new syndicate that took over the property with the idea of converting it into a fashionable international club, whilst retaining its ballroom and refitting the hotel. However, it was not to be, as following the departure of British troops, who occupied the estate during the Sino-Japanese disturbances in 1932, work got under way on redeveloping the site. The Chinese owned Metropole Gardens and Ballroom, one of Shanghai's most popular social and dance venues, took over part of the plot in 1935. Today, nothing is left of that bygone era and much of the site is occupied by West Gate Mall, a skyscraper shopping and commercial complex, and the Majestic Theatre dating from 1941.

Left *The announcement that the Majestic Ballroom was to close came as a shock to Shanghai's social elite*

Opposite *Although the Majestic Hotel had been closed before the Metropole Hotel opened, this advert from the summer of 1930 featured all four hotels that Sassoon operated in Shanghai*

CATHAY MANSIONS
Situated at the corner of Route Cardinal Mercier and Rue Bourgeat, near the Cercle Sportif Francais

MAJESTIC HOTEL
Surrounded by spacious grounds located on Bubbling Well, Gordon, and Avenue Roads

METROPOLE HOTEL
Centrally located near Municipal Building, at Foochow and Kiangse Roads

FOUR LEADING HOTELS IN CHINA

E. CARRARD, General Manager

...an extensive view of the ...iver and environs of the ...he Cathay Hotel contains ..., each with private bath-...pecial ventilating system ...hich washes and cools or ...ing to seasonal require-...rve the Hotel, including ...e top of the building. ...ing Room with spacious ...fortably accommodating ...ddition to this, two com-... and suites of private ...ning rooms. Excepting ...nge, Lobbies and Recep-...Ground Floor, all public ...p part of the building, ...vide terraces.

THE Cathay Mansions is Shanghai's most palatial and best-equipped private Residential Hotel.

The building occupies one of the most desirable residential sites in Shanghai, overlooking the French Club grounds, and with an unsurpassed view of the environs of Shanghai.

Cathay Mansions has the distinction of being the highest and most up-to-date of its kind in the Far East having 280 Rooms and Apartment Suites, all equipped with Private Bathrooms and every modern convenience.

The Main Dining Room is on the eleventh floor with accommodation for 250 people. There are also Private Dining Rooms, and spacious and beautiful Lounges. Additionally, a large Roof Garden, 170 feet above road level, is available for the use of residents and guests, making it the finest Residential Hotel in the Far East.

IDEALLY situated in the heart of the aristocratic Western district, the Majestic Hotel may be said to live up to its regal name in every detail.

Surrounded by extensive gardens, green lawns and flowering shrubs, the guest here enjoys something to be attained at no other hotel in Shanghai, in peaceful outdoor life. In addition to the world-famous ball-room with its attractive orchestra and weekly changes of programme by well-known artists, there are handsome suites of rooms exquisitely furnished, which command views of the gardens. The Majestic also offers many reception rooms, a unique mahjongg room, and the great Empire Banquet Room with its lovely period decoration.

There is also the delightful Italian Garden, amidst myriad lights and feathery trees, where dining and dancing may be indulged in. The Lawn Cinema is another of the Majestic's many attractions.

THE Hotel Metropole, will be known as a "Hotel for businessmen." It is so designed as to be particularly suitable to this type of clientele, authough accommodations are not especially limited to businessmen.

On the ground floor of the hotel will be located the main lounge, reception rooms, general offices, bar and main dining room. In the basement space is to be provided for a grill room, barber shop and luggage rooms. A special feature of the grill room will be a refrigerated air-cooled ventilating system.

The first floor will accommodate a large banquet room, a private dining room and a reception room. Considerable attention is being given to the decorations of these rooms. From the second floor to the fourteenth floor the entire space will be given to bedrooms. Each bedroom will have a bath attached. Suites in the Hotel Metropole will have roof gardens.

...HAY HOTELS, LIMITED. (Arnhold & Company, Limited, General Managers.)

(Incorporated in Hongkong)

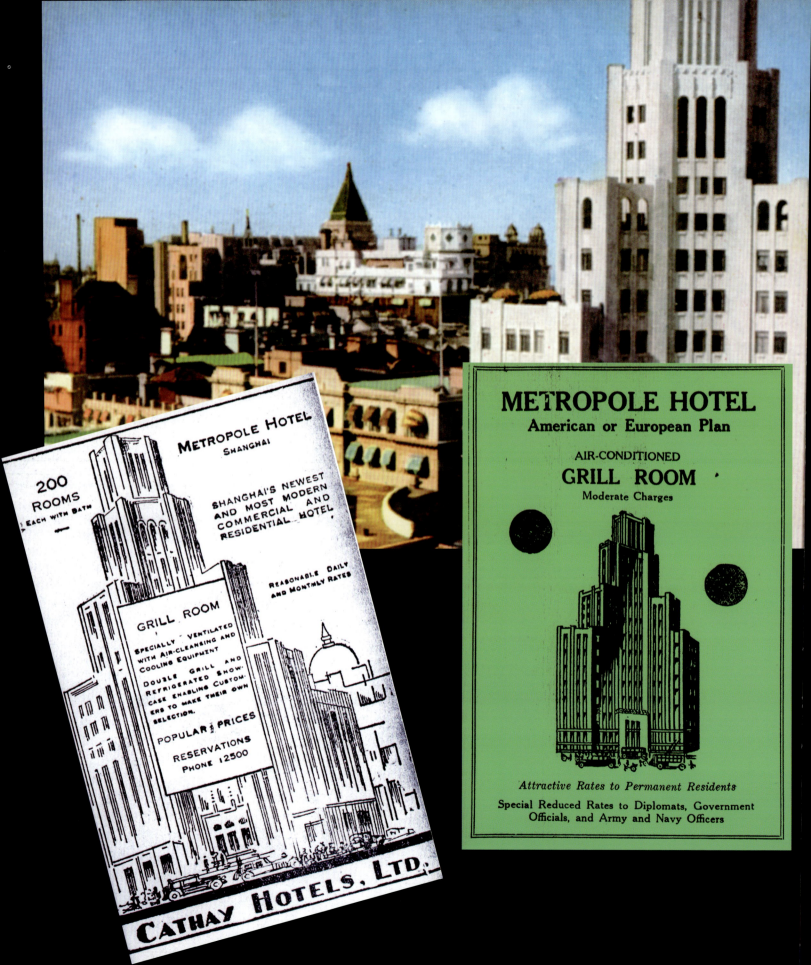

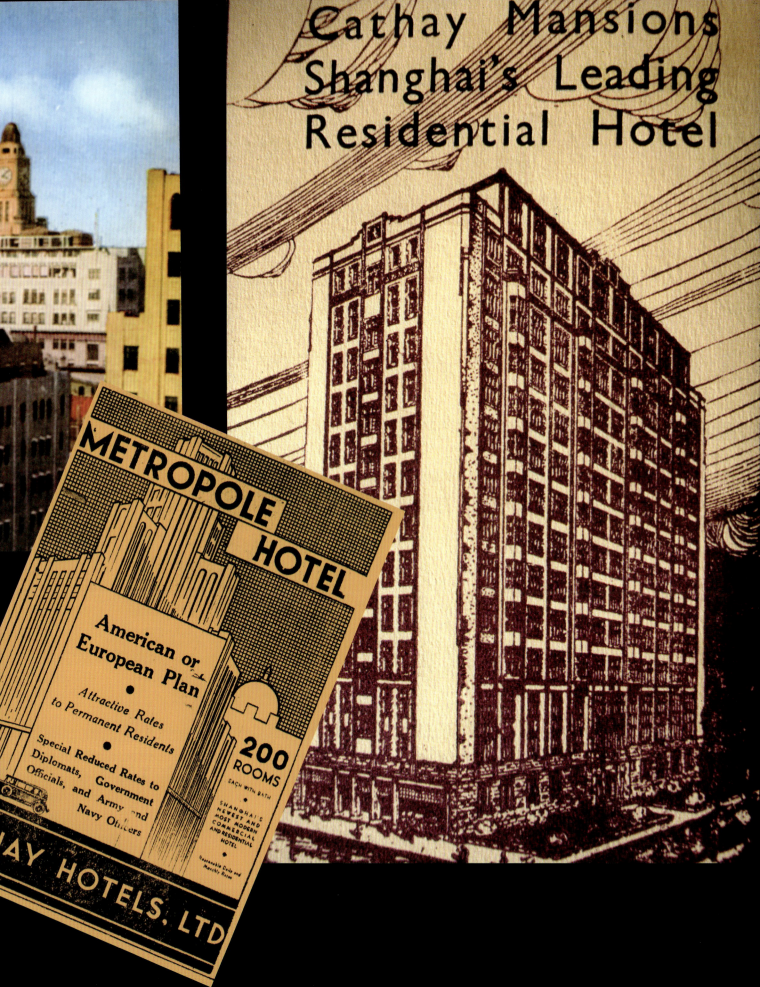

7 | MADE TO ORDER

WITHIN WEEKS OF the Cathay Hotel's opening, word of its superlative cuisine and service, its unique blend of man and machine, had been digested across the Far East. The man came in the form of the rotund and cheerful French head chef, M. Victor Boudard. He had practised his art in the best European hotel and restaurant circles, and would now oversee seventy Chinese cooks, one French chef and one English chef at the Cathay Hotel. The machine came in the form of the most modern kitchen in China, featuring the best of everything – gas ovens, oil ovens, electric stoves, steam vaults, marble slabs, aluminium tables, fiery furnaces and icy caverns. Naturally the pantry was stocked with the finest produce from across the globe – peaches from California, figs from Persia, caviar from Russia, foie gras from Paris, hams from Germany, butter from Australia and cheeses from Italy.

Mr. Guilio Pala, the Italian maitre d'hôtel, who supervised the main dining room, ballroom and the Tower Grill, reportedly found romance, humour and even tragedy over dinner times. Pala had previously been acquainted with popular Swiss manager, Mr. E. Carrard in Europe, and had spent eighteen years at the Cathay Royal on Piccadilly Circus, London. By 1932 the Tower Grill had become one of the most popular restaurants in the Far East, famed for its pukka lunchtime curries created by Indian chefs.

Victor Boudard, Chef de Cuisine

Opposite *The best cuisine for the best people, 1937 advert*

THIS WHITE-APRONED WIZARD PRESIDES OVER A VAST DOMAIN WHERE MODERN INVENTION LENDS ITS AID TO OLD-WORLD CULINARY ART.

The modern voluminous kitchen at the Cathay Hotel, 1929

M. Boudard, with his chief assistant chef, at work in the Cathay Hotel kitchen

The success of the hotel had fully justified the enterprise of Sir Victor Sassoon and his directors who, with foresight and contumacy, had continued with the project despite a battery of criticism from those who pronounced it a white elephant. The hotel was as distinguished as Sir Victor himself, with its character upheld by Carrard and his assistant, Mr. Robert Telfer. Telfer, an American, had previously worked for The Hongkong and Shanghai Hotels, Limited in Shanghai as manager of the Majestic Hotel, and before that at the Astor House Hotel and Palace Hotel. Telfer took over the management of the Cathay Hotel in April 1932, when Carrard was promoted to general manager of the Cathay Hotels, Limited.

Before taking up his new post Carrard took eight months leave in Europe, part of

WHAT'S ON THE MENU?

The Japan Hotel Association, with extensive and impressive interests in Japanese controlled Manchuria, shipped a whole conference of people from Japan to Shanghai in 1935 to see something of the hotel business and exchange ideas for tourist development. For this assemblage of hoteliers the Cathay kitchen produced a voluptuous menu comprising of:

Caviar Gris Perié
Consomme Monaco en Tasse
Delices de Mandarin Waleska
Tournedos Armenoville
Pommes Voisin:
Petits pois fine
Faisan Vendome
Salade Princesse
Mousse Glacée Frou-Frou
Frivolités
Corbeille de Fruits
Café à l' Oriental

which proved to be a 'busman's holiday.' In search of something new to bring back to Shanghai he lodged at Claridges, The Mayfair and The Dorchester in London, and at the new George V Hotel in Paris. He saw nothing beyond what was provided at the Cathay Hotel already. Wishing to return to Europe, Carrard resigned his post in September 1934 and was given a ceremonious send off in the banqueting rooms of the hotel, and presented with a gold watch for his unstinting service.

Indeed, it wasn't long before the hoteliers of the world came to the Cathay Hotel in search of inspiration. The hotel particularly impressed Major Black of the Grosvenor House in London, the largest luxury hotel in the British Empire, during his 1934 visit. He wished to recreate the Peking Room in London, but conceded that without the cheerful Chinese waiters it would lose a great deal of its charm.

CAPON SOUVAROFF

Cook a capon until three-quarters done, then place in a casserole with ½ lb. fois gras and 5 oz. truffles cut into large dice.

Add a little Madeira and the gravy from the capon.

Put the lid on the casserole and seal it firmly to the pot with a strip of paste made of flour and water.

Finish the cooking in a moderate oven for 30 minutes.

The capon must be served in the dish in which it is cooked.

Pheasant or partridge may be substituted for the capon with equal success.

Cathay Hotel recipes from 1941

FILET DE MANDARIN BERCY

Well butter a dish and sprinkle with chopped shallots (or onions).

Arrange on this the fillets of fish. Moisten with a wineglassful of white wine and some of the liquor obtained from the fish bones. Add a lump of butter the size of a walnut and poach in the oven, basting frequently.

When cooked, pour off the liquor into a saucepan and reduce it by half. Stir in some fresh butter and the juice of a lemon, adding chopped parsley. Cover the fillets with this sauce and serve very hot.

CANARD SAUVAGE ROTI—SAUCE ROUENNAISE

While the duck is roasting the sauce is prepared as follows:—

Take: ½ pint red wine,

2 teaspoons chopped shallots (or onions),

Pepper, thyme, and 1 bay leaf,

And reduce to three-quarters of its volume. Add ¾ cup of good brown sauce, and cook for 15 minutes.

Now press through a sieve 4 uncooked duck livers (or chicken livers). Mix with the above sauce and strain.

(On no account must this be allowed to boil, for boiling or intense heat will cause coagulation and ruin the sauce.)

Season to taste, and serve sauce separately.

Opposite *Fine views and fine dining, 1937 advert*

CURRY AT EVES

In 1960, Mary Frost Mabon, food correspondent for *Sports Illustrated* magazine, visited Sir Victor and Lady Sassoon at EVES, their estate in Nassau in the Bahamas, and was treated to Sir Victor's special EVES curry. The recipe appeared in an edition of the magazine on 20 October in that year. Sir Victor recommended a 'half-and-half mixture of Tuborg beer and Bass ale taken ice-cold,' as an accompaniment to cool the throat.

INGREDIENTS:

- 1½ pounds yellow onions
- ½ cup vegetable oil,
- 1 tablespoon turmeric
- Handful fresh parsley leaves,
- 1 pound raw potatoes, pared and cubed
- 4 tablespoons vegetable shortening,
- ½ cup curry powder
- ½ cup vinegar
- 3 dashes Tabasco sauce
- 1½ teaspoons salt
- 1½ packages frozen green beans, cooked
- ½ cup chutney
- ½ cup piccalilli (or chowchow or pickle relish)
- ½ cup tomato ketchup
- ½ cup Worcestershire sauce.
- Dashes of garlic powder and paprika.

PREPARATION AND COOKING:

Start by chopping onions medium coarse and parsley medium fine. Place oil in large heavy stew pan or iron skillet. Mix with onion, turmeric and parsley. Cover and cook extremely slowly, stirring often, till onions are soft. Then stir, uncovered, on medium heat until onions are nicely browned. Mix in ½ teaspoon salt. Place shortening in cold heavy iron fry pan, add raw potato, cook gently for 20 minutes uncovered, stirring often; turn up heat for 5-10 minutes to brown and crust cubes.

Meanwhile, moisten curry powder with vinegar in small bowl, stirring to make a smooth paste and add to the cooked onions. Mix and toss with drained beans over mild heat for five minutes. Add potatoes and previously prepared mixture of remaining ingredients. Also add 1 teaspoon salt. Boil and stir 6 minutes, or till nicely blended.

Thursday was curry day at the Cathay Hotel in 1938

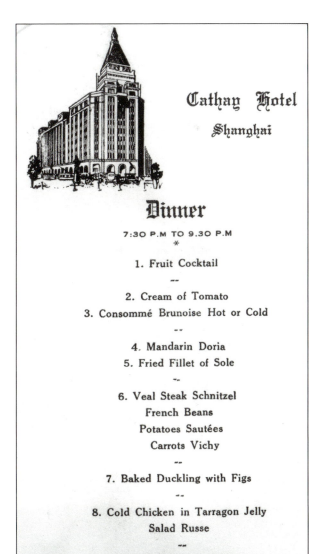

Top Left *Plenty of European favourites on offer for Sunday dinner in 1932*

Top Right *A large replica of the Cathay Hotel made entirely of sugar, 1931*

Bottom Right *Early 1930s luncheon menu*

93

FAST FORWARD – M AT THE PEACE

The Peace Grill in 1989. The room was created in the mid-1980s and occupied part of the former Cathay Hotel eighth-floor lounge.

Michelle Garnaut, restaurateur extraordinaire, opened M on the Bund, in 1999. It's now a legend. However, her first foray into creating fine international cuisine on Shanghai's famous waterfront took place some years earlier in the kitchens of the Peace Hotel. Garnaut had stayed at the Peace Hotel on numerous occasions in the early 1990s, but is was on a 1995 visit, when accompanied by Bruno van der Burg, her manager of M at The Fringe in Hong Kong, that he suggested opening a restaurant in the city.

In September 1996, she was back at the hotel with Hong Kong-based Ted Marr, who had already arranged two huge and very successful parties at the hotel. He was working on staging a 'Handover Ball' at the hotel as part of a series of events culminating in Hong Kong on 30 June 1997. When they met the Peace Hotel management to discuss food and beverage arrangements, Garnaut spontaneously asked Mr. Wang, the general manager, if she could come and cook in the hotel. Despite an initial reluctance, he finally agreed to allow Garnaut to prepare a feast for him and 11 others. Such was the success of the meal (with most of the ingredients and dishes being brought up from Hong

Kong), that Garnaut was invited back to cook for the public in the Peace Grill on the hotel's eighth floor. She and four of her team came up from Hong Kong for 11 days in December 1996, for what she described as 'a nerve-racking experience.' However, it was a remarkable success as the restaurant, which was accustomed to hosting only a handful of guests, attracted 50 people a night. With the episode behind her, Garnaut decided to start the hunt for her own restaurant in Shanghai in March 1997.

Her menu for the Peace Hotel included, among other delicacies, chestnut soup laced with olive oil, Crêpes Parmentier topped with cured salmon caviar and sour cream, and Porcini fettuccine with mushrooms, pea leaves and Parma ham for starters. Mains included slowly baked salt-encased selected leg of lamb with roasted root vegetables and creamed spinach, bone roasted plump pigeon studded with truffle and artichokes on soft polenta, and the Mayor of Nice's braised oxtail with Provençal mashed potatoes and Jesse's carrots. The meal could be rounded off with desserts including pavlova and sticky toffee pudding with a rich butterscotch sauce.

An advert for the 11-day culinary adventure

95

Canadian Pacific Liner. "EMPRESS OF BRITAIN."
KNICKERBOCKER BAR.

8 FOUR-MINUTE GUESTS

IN THE EARLY 1920s, Shanghai experienced a huge upsurge in the number of visiting tourists, when the major shipping lines with their magnificent cruise-liners, including the *Belgenland*, the *Franconia*, the *Resolute* and the *Empress of Britain*, began to call at the city on their circumnavigation of the globe. Many of the larger liners would dock at Woosung (Wusong), near the confluence of the Yangtze (Yangzi) and Whangpoo (Huangpu) rivers. Others would dock near the Astor House Hotel, not far from the Bund. It was not uncommon for 400 or more eager sightseers to be discharged and relayed in smaller craft to the Bund at one time. Gingerly alighting from their tenders at the Customs Jetty, in front of the Custom House with its clock, 'Big Ching', imitating the chimes of Big Ben at Westminster, the European buildings on the Bund would confound the visitor anxiously looking for a fictitious opium-smoking pigtailed Chinaman. They were more likely to bump into a fellow American, wishing to catch up with news

from home. The Bund presented a Western face to visitors, who were usually in some part surprised, bemused, exhilarated or disappointed by its appearance. For many it was their first taste of China and there were no temples or pagodas in sight.

By the early 1930s Shanghai was playing host to around 40,000, largely rich American, globetrotters each year. Most round-the-world tourists would spend just one or two days in the city and the Shanghailanders, the city's foreign resident population, often referred to them as 'four-minute guests.' A 1934 guidebook, *All About Shanghai*, informed its readers that the Bund was 'the natural starting point for any tour of Shanghai, for it is here that a large majority of newcomers to Shanghai first step foot in the city.' The world-girdlers would set off from its promenade in a cavalcade of motor vehicles on carefully crafted itineraries that were designed not to disappoint by presenting images of China in Western-style comfort. Their exhaustive itineraries, apart from sightseeing, took in

Opposite *Travelling in style, the Empress of Britain was a frequent visitor to Shanghai in the 1920s*

the sensual delights that were Shanghai's tour de force – shopping, dining, dancing and entertainment. In many ways their Shanghai sojourn was an intensified form of their cruise-ship routine where entertainment during the long sea passages took the form of bridge parties, screenings of the latest talking pictures, games, frolics and contests of all kinds, as well as dancing and masquerades. As such, the sights of Shanghai held little interest for some visitors, who were more concerned with hobnobbing and having as much indulgent fun as time would allow. For some, this meant staying within the confines of the Cathay Hotel till the ship embarked. The following sketch, printed in the *North-China Herald* in 1937, nicely summed up the sentiment:

> Yes, Mary Louise, I must say I think a lot more of Shanghai than I did when I got on the tender this morning. Why, I almost took the advice of that Miss Know-it-All who didn't think it worthwhile to come up to the port at all. 'Shanghai's not China' says she. Well maybe not, but there's plenty Chinese here, anyway. And the Cathay Hotel. Can you beat it anywhere? I just loved their dining room and this lounge.
>
> How you ever get time to have your hair marcelled, Mary Louise, in all this excitement!

Opposite *Shanghai had little to learn from her wealthy foreign tourists when it came to fashion. Pages from the Shanghai press, early 1930s.*

In safe foreign hands. American Express were masters of making travellers feel at home in Shanghai since 1918

– Oh, you made a date with Captain Williamses wife, and she took you to her favourite hotel, the Palace. Yes, all the Navy people and lots of other folk I met before I sailed told me I must go there if I got the chance. And then after 'elevenses' – do Shanghai people eat every hour of the day? – she took you up to the Bond Street Salon right in the building and you were beautified then and there. And such a smart style, too. I've half a mind to go there instead of seeing the Pagoda this afternoon.

Any way, let's do a little shopping before the party sets out. Will you come along? I've some good addresses. We'll get the clerk to get us some real nice rickshaw men that can speak American and know where the bargains are.

Travel agents Thomas Cook and American Express established in Shanghai in 1910 and 1918, respectively, offered an assortment of tours for the four-minuters. Typically they would begin with a visit to the Native City, taking in a cup of tea at the Willow Pattern Tea House and a stroll through the Mandarin's (Yu) Garden and the bird market, with time allowed for curio shopping in its frenzied, colourful, bazaar. Then, it would be back to the Peking Room at the hotel for lunchtime tiffin. In the afternoon, visits to St. John's Church or the Siccawei (Xujiahui) Observatory and Convent, and perhaps the

A BIG BUILDING?

'Eee Lad', said one. 'That's a tall building'. 'Nay it's na so big' replied the sceptic in the party. 'Dussent thou think it's a big building, Jake?' the first observer appealed to another mate. 'Aye, it's a big building,' Jake replied. 'It's not so big', maintained the sceptic. 'Well, lad, it seems it's a big building', the first speaker went on conceding a point. 'It's na such a big building as it seems', replied the sceptic scoring a direct hit. 'It looks like a big building', suggested Jake tentatively. 'It's na so big as it looks, lad', the opponent went on. 'This is na England remember'. This unanswerable argument was enough for the first observer. 'Aye, may be you're right. It's not such a big building after all.'

An account from the North-China Daily News, *30 March 1931, on how a group of soldiers from the Northumberland Fusiliers perceived their first sight of the Cathay Hotel.*

Lunghwa (Longhua) Pagoda and Jessfield (Zhongshan) Park, would feature before returning to the hotel for the tea dance, which ceremoniously marked the early onset of nightfall and a passage to the city's peerless blaze of nightlife. That's when the real sightseeing began.

American Express offered a night tour that kicked-off with a feast of shark's fin and bird's nest soup in a high-class Chinese restaurant, usually on Foochow (Fuzhou) Road, followed by a visit to the nearby Great World Amusement Centre – an entertainment palace with four floors of stages and booths for plays, acrobatics,

Early 1930s visitors to Shanghai travelling on the Resolute

CHINESE AND GENTLEMEN

The Cathay Hotel advertised itself as an international establishment, welcoming both Chinese and foreign patronage. Yet 1933 saw a storm blow up over a tongue-in-cheek accusation by a Chinese customer. In a letter to a Shanghai magazine, dated 17 August:

Apparently out of its appreciation for the generous high Chinese Officials the Cathay Hotel has provided lavatories specially marked for 'Chinese' while for Foreigners its lavatories are reserved for 'Gentlemen.' We may suggest that the Hotel Management build a chute from its Cashiers counter to the Whangpoo, so that the money of the undesirable Chinese may be dumped into that river. It just can't be clean enough to mix with the coins turned in by 'White' hands.

In fact the accusation wasn't strictly true as the lavatories were only so differentiated in Sassoon House and not the hotel. However it left the Chinese, who had been treated as both Chinese and gentlemen in Peking, Paris or London, in somewhat of a predicament. Which door were they entitled or expected to enter? Shortly after, the signs were changed to read 'Gentlemen' and 'Staff', placing another predicament in the path of those Chinese who received salaries.

How did those accustomed to thinking of themselves as gentlemen and Chinese fathom these Westerners' ways? Were they required to assume a dual identity? They understood the term gentleman as referring to well-bred, honourable men and the word Chinese as simply referring to a native of China. One did not exclude the other. But gentleman also implied membership of the upper classes. Certainly not all Westerners in Shanghai were so attached and those who were, or pretended to be, often felt ashamed of Shanghai's large poor White Russian population. If not of the gentry, foreigners in the International Settlement were endemically privileged, poor Russians excluded of course. In categorically solving the riddle one Chinese gentleman writer concluded that 'gentleman' when used as a form of address implied politeness and often this seemed unnecessary to the Chinese in Shanghai.

The story of Lu Xun's reception at the Cathay Hotel is still popularly recounted today. China's most famous man of letters, dressed in a blue cotton gown and wearing rubber shoes, had to walk up to the seventh floor of the hotel to visit a British friend after being denied the use of the lift by an attendant. On being shown to the lift to go back down by his friend, the attendant, looking embarrassed, allowed him in. Lu Xun, apparently, found the whole episode rather amusing.

singing and feats of magic, as well as penny arcades and galleries of horrors. The next stop was the roof garden at the Sincere Department Store on Nanking (Nanjing) Road for Chinese theatricals and sing-song girl routines. The tour ended with revellers being dropped off, just before 11.00 p.m., at one of the city's famous foreign cabarets – the Venus Cafe, Del Montes, the Vienna Gardens, or the ultra-modern and chic Ciro's – the latter being yet another of Sir Victor Sassoon's interests.

The management of the Cathay Hotel were always delighted to receive such large groups of relatively unimposing guests, as were the curio, silk, lace and embroidery dealers in the Sassoon House Arcade for whom Christmas came many times a year. Likewise the rickshaw coolie, described by a reporter for the *North-China Herald* as a 'most conscientious and enterprising breed,' was able to capitalise on the naivety of the stranger by making outrageous demands for money, often unquestioned, or, if challenged, to be met by a blank face or a diatribe of incomprehensible moans and wails. The tourist

The Paris of the East. Fashion page from one of the many foreign newspapers printed in Shanghai

103

Shanghai's ultra-sophisticated and first modern nightclub, owned by Sir Victor Sassoon and designed by Palmer & Turner architects, opened in 1936. Adverts from 1937.

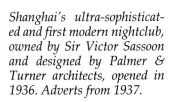

though for some they were a source of annoyance, resentment and jealousy. Accusations were frequently made that Shanghai's wealthy and ostentatious visitors contributed to the rising cost of living in the city. However, few of the resident British population had any qualms over tourists being charged over the odds as they, especially the Americans, was also prey to the petty criminal and pickpocket, with many, usually of Russian blood, having been reportedly caught in the act in the Cathay Hotel lobby.

Most Shanghailanders viewed the tourists as a harmless form of amusement,

Popular Russian cartoonist Sapajou joyfully depicts the consequences of the night before

were often regarded as small-minded and over-affluent 'suckers.' Some British passengers on the American dominated liners often shared the same opinion. One such passenger on the Red Star liner *Belgenland*, commented on the Americans as 'being awful people who of course pay anything they are asked right away, so prices have gone up – three or four times more than usually asked, and they ask eight times more than they will give you things for, so the Americans pay about 30 times too much.'

In some ways, Shanghailanders and the world-girdlers shared a similar predicament. Whilst confined on board ship, passengers would form a small, isolated community that could be compared to that of the British community in Shanghai, which itself often moved in small and isolated circles. Visitors popularly believed that Shanghai's foreign community was narrow-minded, grasping and incapable of seeing any good in the Chinese. And there was no doubt that they were under scrutiny from those world-wise travellers looking to glory in their superior mores, and quick to dismiss people and places as old-fashioned and obsolete. However, when it came to the Cathay Hotel, they had to think again.

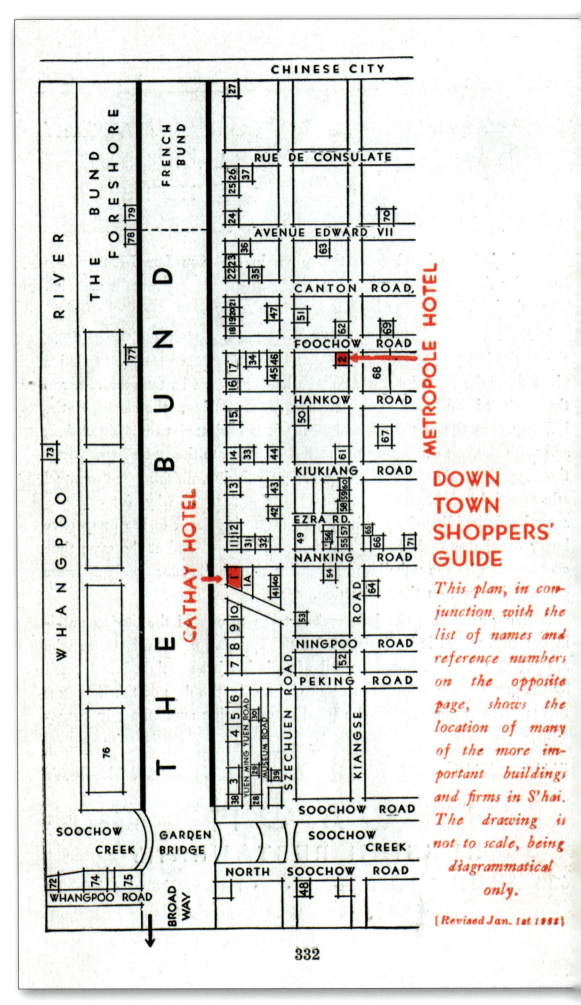

106

Down Town Shoppers' Guide

Plan Reference

	Ref.
HOTELS	
Cathay Hotel & Sassoon Bldg.	1
Metropole Hotel	2
BANKS	
American Express	60
American-Oriental Bank	32
Bank of China	10
Bank of Communications	15
Bank of Taiwan	13
Banque de l'Indo-Chine	5
Banque Franco-Chinoise	24
Chartered Bank of India	12
Chase Bank, The	43
Central Bank of China	14
Commercial Bank of China	20
Cook & Son, Bankers Ltd., Thos.	49
Deutsch Asiatische Bank	44
Hongkong & Shanghai Bank	17
Mercantile Bank of India	8
National City Bank of N.Y.	33
Netherlands' Trading Society	1A
P. & O. Banking Corporation	20
Yokohama Specie Bank	9

PUBLIC BUILDINGS, UTILITIES, ETC.

	Ref.
British Consulate General	3
Chinese General Post Office	48
Chinese Passport Office	63
Chinese Radio Administration	1A
Chinese Telegraph Office	46
Custom House	16
Custom's Examination Depot	77
Eastern Extension Telegraph Co.	36
French Consulate	37
French Semaphone & Signal Station	79
German Consulate	74
Great Northern Telegraph Co.	36
Hamilton House	62
Japanese Consulat	72
Municipal Administration Building	68
Netherlands Consulate General opp.	37
Norwegian Consulate	47
Pootung Point Signal Station	73
Public Gardens	76
Shanghai War Memorial	78
Soviet Consulate	75
United States Consulate	61

TRAVEL BUREAUS

	Ref.
American Express	60
China National Aviation Corporation	35
China Travel Service	41
Cook & Son, Ltd., Thos.	49
Japan Tourist Burau	54

SHIPPING OFFICES

	Ref.
Anglo-Danish Shipping Co.	25
Butterfield & Swire	27
Canadian Pacific Steamships	22
China Merchants S. N. Co.	18
China Navigation Co.	27
Cook & Son, Ltd., Thos.	49
Dairen Kisen Kaisha	47
Dollar Steamship Lines	35
Glen & Shire Lines S.S.	6
Jardine, Matheson & Co., Ltd.	7
Java-China-Japan-Line	51
Lloyd Triestno	62
Messageries Maritimes	26
Nippon Yusen Kaisha	4
Nisshin Kisen Kaisha	21
P. & O. S. N. Co.	22
States Steamship Co.	62
Yangtsze Rapids S.S. Co.	17

CLUBS

	Ref.
American Club	69
Shanghai Club	23

CHURCHES

	Ref.
Cathedral, Holy Trinity. (C. of England)	67
Union Church	38
American Community Ch.	

DOWN TOWN

Sassoon Arcade

	Ref.
Gray's Yellow Lantern	1A

Central Arcade

	Ref.
Fette Rug Cc.	49
Handcrafts	49
Peking Treasure Shop	49
Sea Captain's Shop	49
Shanghai Kerchief Store	49
The Modern	49
Toyo Murakami	58

	Ref.
Aquarius Co.	34
Baroukh	64
"Cathay" Magazine	39
Caldbeck, MacGregor & Co., Ltd.	34
Eastman Kodak Co.	29
Fine Arts Studio, 1147 Bubb. Well Rd.	
Francis Beauty Salon	62
Jardine Matheson (*Spirits*)	7
Josephine C. Gowns	30
McMichael, E. H.	56
Millington Ltd.	39

333

Opposite *Visitor's guide to the area around the Cathay and Metropole Hotels from the Cathay Magazine, 1932*

Much
All good
Wishes to all Video
Antonio
Sincerely
Bert Wheeler
Mentionobey

9 CELEBRITIES AT THE CATHAY

THE CATHAY HOTEL courted celebrities from all walks of life. The hotel's most famed guest, or at least the one whose name recurs in print with routine regularity, was Noel Coward. Coward, apparently in an effort to ease a state of mental anguish, took to the seas from San Francisco on the *President Garfield* in November 1929 and dreamed up the idea for his smash hit play *Private Lives* a few weeks later in Yokohama. Coward's ideas for the play ripened while he was confined with flu to an English suite at the hotel at the end of December, and as he convalesced 'propped up in bed with a writing-block and an Eversharp pencil,' the script was summarily completed within roughly four days.

Having cast off the flu and the script, Coward recounted that he 'entered the social whirl of Shanghai with zest. There were lots of parties and Chinese dinners and general cosmopolitan junketings, which, while putting a slight strain on our lingual abilities, in no way dampened our spirits. We found some charming new friends, notably Madame Birt and her twin daughters who, apart from being extremely attractive, could quarrel with each other in six different languages without even realising that they were not sticking to one; and three English naval officers, Ascherson, Bushell and Guerrier, with whom we visited many of the lower and gayer haunts of the city.' Coward left Shanghai on a naval ship, the *HMS Suffolk*, for Hong Kong where he spent another week typing and revising *Private Lives* in his room at The Peninsula hotel.

On a return visit in 1936, Coward, a fan of Chinese talking pictures and personal friend of China's most famous opera star, Mei Lanfang, was working on his autobiography. Coward's last sojourn at the Cathay Hotel was totally unplanned. His ship, the *Monterey*, was diverted on its way from California to Australia to pick up foreign evacuees from the city in November 1940. After taking on board many Shanghailanders, including a large contingent of children from the Shanghai

Opposite *Hollywood stars Bert Wheeler and Bob Woolsey stayed at the Cathay Hotel in 1933*

American School, Coward, who was on his way to Australia on a goodwill mission, confined himself to his cabin, only venturing out for the late dinner call or for coffee and liqueurs in a quiet corner with his group of friends. Among other Hollywood stars, Ronald Coleman, one of Coward's greatest friends, also stayed at the hotel.

Both Douglas Fairbanks and his wife Mary Pickford fell in love with Shanghai upon their first visit in 1929 when they stayed at the Majestic Hotel, just before its operation was taken over by the Cathay Hotels, Limited. On that occasion they spent nearly a week in the city, with Pickford telling a reporter from the

Shanghai Times that it was 'the world's greatest shopping centre,' adding that 'I say that from experience.' The couple made a return visit in February 1931 on board the *SS Belgenland* that allowed them just 19 hours in the city. Pressed for time, Fairbanks arrived two hours late at a reception in the Cathay Hotel given in his honour by United Artists' local distributor. Some of the several hundred guests had already given up in despair and gone home. Fairbanks, however, found some redemption by paying a glowing tribute to Shanghai, saying, 'to me there are only five prominent cities in the world and Shanghai in my opinion occupies the limelight as the most colourful and interesting and progressive.' Following his separation from Pickford, Fairbanks returned to Shanghai for a golf tournament in 1932, and on his fifth visit in 1935 he spent his entire day ashore at Sir Victor Sassoon's villa.

One of Fairbank's oldest and greatest friends, Charles Chaplin, who was acquainted with Sir Philip Sassoon, Victor's cousin and the youngest member of the British Parliament, caused a splash when he stayed at the hotel for just one night in March 1936. Accompanied by Paulette Goddard, amidst rumours of their engagement and a commotion surrounding his epochal movie *Modern Times*, they

Charlie Chaplin meets Chinese opera legend Mei Lanfang on his 1936 visit

PANDA AT THE PALACE HOTEL

Perhaps the most famous celebrity guest ever to stay at the Palace Hotel was not a prince, nor even a person, but a baby panda named Su-Lin! It was a story that made sensational international headlines.

Ruth Harkness, a New York fashionista, was Su-Lin's most unlikely foster mother. Just days after being found in the hollow of a spruce tree deep in the heart of Sichuan Province, Harkness and Su-Lin, the only live panda in captivity, flew to Shanghai and checked in at the Palace Hotel in December 1937. They stayed in the room that had been occupied by her adventurer husband Bill when he set upon an expedition to capture a live panda in early 1935. Following his death in February 1936 Harkness, more accustomed to highballs and haute-couture in fashionable Manhattan, took up the call to the wilds and teamed up with a dashing Chinese American explorer named Quentin Young to continue his mission. Jack, Quentin's brother, had accompanied Theodore and Kermit Roosevelt, sons of the former American president, on the first successful foreign hunt for a panda in 1929. It was later stuffed and exhibited in Chicago's Field Museum.

In complete contrast, Su-Lin was very much alive, and enjoyed the warmth from the fireplace in Harkness's room at the hotel during the cold winter of 1936. Two friends, prominent Shanghai businessmen Mr. Floyd James and Mr. Fritz Hardenbrooke, took turns to nanny and feed the cub. Mr. Hardenbrooke took a room across from Mrs. Harkness, where the panda slept on alternate nights. Su-Lin was reported to have kept 'regular hours', sleeping most of the time and waking and crying when hungry.

The hotel became their home for two weeks as Harkness battled to get permission to get the panda out of the country and into an American zoo, whilst attempting to remain incognito. The Palace Hotel staff was asked not to reveal Harkness's whereabouts or any of her plans. But the news spread fast. One local newspaper, the *China Press*, reported that the hotel had begun to look like 'a Zoologist Association Conference,' rather than a 'Bundside hostelry.' Despite many anxious moments, Harkness left Shanghai on 2 December 1936, on board the liner *President McKinley* bound for San Francisco. In her hand she held a voucher for 'one dog, $20.00.'

The duo caused a sensation upon their return to America and Su-Lin found a new home at Chicago's Brookfield Zoo. The zoo funded Harkness's return trip in her quest to capture yet another panda. She checked into her old room at the Palace Hotel just days before a bomb hit the building on 14 August 1937. Harkness escaped unhurt, having ignored a good friend's advice to stay in the hotel for her own safety. Unlikely as it was, she found what she came for in December with the purchase of a panda from Chinese hunters. Baby panda Mei-mei and Harkness said goodbye to the Palace Hotel and to Shanghai on January 28, 1938.

However, it wasn't going to be Harkness's last visit to her beloved country. She returned in 1938, following the death of Su-Lin, and with the help of Quentin Young captured another panda as a companion for Mei-mei. After months of trying to settle the cub in Sichuan province, Harkness decided to set the animal free and returned alone from what was to be her last voyage from Shanghai.

Top *Ruth Harkness and Su-Lin in front of the fireplace in her room at the Palace Hotel*

Bottom *Floyd James and Fritz Hardenbrooke with Su-Lin*

were besieged by Shanghai's foreign and Chinese press corps. George Vanderbilt and his wife, who were on a roaming honeymoon, were staying in the hotel when the couple arrived.

The first thing that Chaplin did when he entered the Cathay Suite was to ask for the plants to be removed. That accomplished, he sat down to face some thirty journalists wanting to know what associations *Modern Times* had with communism. Chaplin was emphatic in denying any such argument. The film received its gala première just five days before Chaplin's departure from the States, and his hope that the trip would remove him from the hullabaloo had obviously backfired. He was left exhausted by the questioning and categorically refused to comment on his alleged engagement to Miss Goddard. Although Chaplin was closely guarded, some curio and antique dealers managed get into his suite. On a happier note, Chaplin met up with his old friend Mei Lanfang. His Shanghai experience also spawned an idea for a story based on the life of a White Russian Countess, working as a taxi dancer in the city. Chaplin worked on developing the script, which he called *Stowaway*, during his return to America. However it wasn't until 1967 that the story was brought to the silver screen as *A Countess from Hong Kong*.

Bert Wheeler and Bob Woolsey, two star Hollywood comedians, also stayed at the Cathay Hotel in May 1933. Whitey Smith, former bandleader at the Majestic Hotel, who had made their acquaintance on a ship en route from Osaka to Shanghai, escorted them to the hotel. In his hilarious book, *I Didn't Make a Million*, Smith tells that one of the assembled fans presented Woolsey with a table radio. Later, whilst in their suite, Smith suggested that they listen to some music and Woolsey asked if it would be all right to play the radio. Smith

Marquis Marconi

thought that would be fine, but as he recalled 'he plugged it in and it blew up in his face. The current in Shanghai is 220-V and this was an American radio 110-V. If looks could kill, I would be buried.'

Just months later, a very distinguished guest in the form of the inventor of the wireless, Marquis Marconi, stayed in the Cathay Suite at the hotel. Huge crowds greeted Marconi, his wife and other members of his party, including H. E. Comm. R. Bosecrarelli, the Italian Minister to China, upon their arrival in Shanghai. At a reception organised by the Pan-Pacific Association, its president and the Nationalist Minister of Finance, H. H. Kung, remarked the Marconi was 'a romantic hero in the realm of science,' and that 'mankind owes him a debt of gratitude.' While in Shanghai, Marconi visited the first Marconi beam wireless station in China, which was being tested at nearby Chenju. The station opened in February 1934, allowing direct radio communication between Britain and China.

When in need, H. H. Kung's brother-in-law, Generalissimo Chiang Kai-shek, would visit his dentist, Dr. Daniel J. Collins, in Sassoon House. However, more often than not, Dr. Collins would be flown around China on the general's private plane to administer treatment, with Madame Chiang Kai-shek, also a patient, acting as translator.

Maharajahs, royalty, and diplomats came and went. His Highness Maharaja Sir Sayaji Rao III, the Gaekwar of Baroda, who was reported to enjoy billiards, tennis, shooting and tiger hunting, stayed on his round the world tour in 1933. In the same year other regal guests included the Earl of Aylesford and Prince Karl of Sweden, nephew of King Gustav V. Sir Alexander Cadogan, British Minister to China and his sister Lady Sophie Scott stayed in 1934, at the same time that Sir Eric and Lady Teichman were in residence. Teichman, a

Marquis and Marchioness Marconi at Jiaotong University, 1933

113

consular official, was also a renowned explorer and author of books on Tibet and Turkistan. His Highness the Maharajah of Karpurthala, one of India's leading princes, stayed in the hotel's Indian suite in 1939.

And when it came to the rich, there was no richer girl in the world than Doris Duke Cromwell, the American tobacco heiress, who stayed at the Cathay in 1935 on the sixth month of her honeymoon tour with her husband James Cromwell, a noted American economist and political commentator. The 22-year-old Mrs. Cromwell had inherited a fortune in excess of US$30,000,000. Their marriage lasted until 1943 and, at the time of her death in 1993, her estate was valued at well in excess of a billion dollars. Mr. Kikumoto, an influential Japanese financier, and Yukie, his thoroughly modern golf-playing daughter, also stayed at the hotel in 1935. Another 'modern woman' to pay a visit that year

The Maharaja of Karpurthala and entourage at dinner in the Cathay Hotel Tower, April 1939

Doris Duke Cromwell, the richest girl in the world, and her husband on their 1935 visit

was Yolanda Chen, daughter of four-time Nationalist Minister of Foreign Affairs Eugene Chen and the only Chinese cinematographer in the world.

The hotel itself was cast centre stage in Vicki Baum's 1939 novel *Shanghai '37* (or *Nanking Road*, the British edition title), based on the tragedies of war experienced in the city in 1937. Despite an assurance in the foreword to a 1986 reprint, which comes with a stylised image of the Cathay Hotel on the cover, that the hotel and Baum's fictitious 'Shanghai Hotel' were one and the same, the latter was a hybrid of fact and fiction.

Opening Night

THE
DI GAETANO
GIRLS

•

Cathay
Hotel
Ballroom

•

HARRIS
and YVONNE
ASHBURN

10 | ON THE TOWN

THE FOREIGN POPULATION exhaustively searched for amusement in Shanghai, perhaps with more gusto than that found in any other city around the globe. Hotels and dance halls thrived on Shanghai's joie de vivre, a roly-poly of excessive eating, drinking and dancing. And the fun wasn't just reserved for the gentlemen, as Shanghai's foreign womenfolk, with club life at the root of their existence, would be on a continual round of dinner parties, dancing and jazz nights at the hotels. A self-indulgent lust for pleasure was the hallmark of foreign life in Shanghai's modern society and the Cathay Hotel provided the ultimate venue for life's sensual pleasures.

The Cathay Hotel thrived on entertainment – from musical folly to sombre classical concerts, from fanciful tea dances and impromptu cocktail parties to full-blown pious balls. And, of course, Sir Victor's private parties. There were all manner of events for the social elite, the favoured, the opportune, and for the passing world tourist apt to dispense with a stock of dollars in excess of the number of minutes spoiled in Shanghai.

The opening of the Cathay Hotel coincided with a move by the Shanghai Municipal Council to improve law, order and public morals in the International Settlement. In the face of increased drunken behaviour on the streets, the Council had restricted opening hours of public places of entertainment until just two in the morning, with a discretionary extension available for the favoured. Public opinion was largely against the move, which many saw as a way of protecting the taipans' interests, by restricting the ignominious practise of chit signing and softening the damage caused by staff arriving for work the next morning with sore heads.

The Cathay Ballroom and the Tower Night Club were at the centre of a row in 1935, when police investigations were launched into the habit of the management of keeping open house until four in the morning on Sundays. In fact Mr.

Opposite *Opening nights, like this one in 1935, were gala affairs attended by the cream of Shanghai society*

Capt. P. H. Call.

Sir Victor Sassoon
Requests your presence
at
School and Supper
on January 19th at 10.0 p.m.

Cathay Hotel,
Dancing.

R.S.V.P.
Mrs. P. A. Montgomery
Secretary.

Carrard had cancelled their licence extension before he left Shanghai in 1934, though his successor Mr. Louis Suter, who had previously managed London's Hotel Claridge and Shepheard's Hotel in Cairo, pleaded innocent to knowledge of this fact. In the end Suter had to admit his error and was forced to apply for another licence as well as pay 'arrears' for the numerous occasions on which the law had been broken.

Left *A personal invitation from Sir Victor Sassoon shows the action didn't start until late*

Right *Host, Sir Victor Sassoon, at one of his Shipwreck parties in 1935*

Posing for a photo at one of Sir Victor Sassoon's legendary Circus Parties, February 1935

No such laws applied to private entertaining, which Sir Victor so generously and extravagantly provided in his eleventh-floor suite. He was widely renowned for his fancy dress parties, often bordering on the bizarre and perverse, in the Cathay Ballroom. At his shipwreck party in 1933 he donned blue trousers, beret and scarlet shirt, and dangled a hot water bottle from his waist. Shanghai's most respected citizens, wearing nightgowns and pyjamas, ambled round the hotel half-clad, finding courage in a cocktail glass as well as in the absurdity of their dress. *The North-China Daily News* picked out Mary Hayley Bell, for her courage in wearing a flannel nightdress with her hair in curlers, looking 'very much prettier than most girls could in that dress.' Hayley Bell, the daughter of a colonel who worked as a Chinese Maritime Customs official, was to meet her future husband, the late Sir John Mills, whilst he was on tour with the Quaints Theatre Group in Shanghai.

Despite rumours that Sir Victor was to cut back on his entertaining, the 1934 party season kicked off in January with a schoolroom frolic, with guests being invited to dress for a school and supper party. The Cathay Ballroom was transformed into

Scenes from Sir Victor Sassoon's Circus Party, February 1935

a giant classroom complete with blackboards, maps and other instruments of learning. The orchestra promenaded old school songs, whilst children's games including musical chairs and ring of roses added an element of rough and tumble. Very much at the head, Sir Victor, frocked in a gown with mortarboard, yielded a formidable birch cane to all those that came in range! A circus party was thrown soon after, with guests appearing as seals, donkeys and circus acts including a tattooed lady. Sir Victor ruled over events in a scarlet ringmaster's coat – this time wielding a whip!

Sassoon also had a passion for entertaining the young folk of Shanghai. In February 1937 the ballroom was transformed into a toyshop, where several hundred of Shanghai's privileged progenies gathered dressed as toys. A few days later some of his older friends were invited to a reception and dancing party at the same venue, in the same spirit. On that occasion

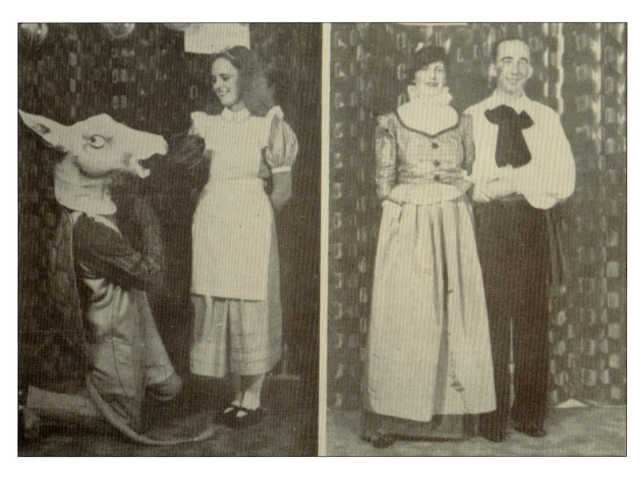

Guests at a 1937 Toy Party

THE PALACE PERSONALITY

Off to the Palace

Conveniently located near the Customs Jetty and right in the centre of the hustle and bustle of the town Mrs. Palace holds open house for her friends. Her front door is always full of people coming and going, her luggage entrance is always busy. One might think that she would be glad to lead a quieter life for she is not as young as she once was and there are those who claim to see silver threads among the gold of her well marcelled hair. But no excitement is the breath of life to her and she delights in the fact that her comfortable lounges are always full.

Long and favourably known, not only throughout the length and breadth of China, but all over the world, Mrs. Palace delights in showing her friends her spacious lobby, with its well proportioned staircase and handsome panelling, in setting before them highly superior coffee and tea, for which crowds flock for elevenses and five-o'clocks every day, to say nothing of noon-time rendezvous and quick, but delicious snacks. All Shanghai looks upon Mrs. Palace as a popular hostess, enjoys her recitals in the lounge and would not know what to do with itself were her hospitable doors not open.

North-China Daily News, 15 January 1936

the *North-China Daily News* reported that 'with many dinner parties preceding it Sir Victor Sassoon's reception and ball held in the Cathay Ballroom was last night's outstanding social event. More than 300 guests, including representatives of practically every nationality attended the affair which began at 10 p.m. and continued until the early morning hours.' Though never taken for granted, the parties, which were such a natural and routine feature of Shanghai high-life, spurred only minimal recognition in the busy social columns of the Shanghai press.

With Sir Victor's frequent comings and goings, to oversee his foreign business concerns or to preside over his racing establishment in India, each departure and return called for yet another round of revelry. The Shanghai swirl never ceased and Sassoon continued to entertain in lavish style right up until his departure in early 1941.

Occasionally, private parties would be held much in the same vein as Sir Victor's affairs at the Cathay Hotel. Such events were very popular among Shanghai's younger American set, some of whom once appeared as a horde of scavengers, importing a complete roadside Chinese kitchen into the ballroom whilst amusing themselves with a treasure hunt for live chickens, cockroaches and frogs. The

Caloris and Mia Monna and Frank Alexander and Elizabeth Swanson wooed the Cathay crowd in 1934

hotel's most famous resident, Dr. Anne Walter Fearn, a self proclaimed 'museum specimen' of Shanghai, regularly hosted dinner and bridge parties, and a host of other entertainments for her wide circle of friends.

The Cathay Ballroom became Shanghai's premier Saturday night venue following the closure of the famed Majestic Hotel Ballroom in 1930. On such nights Sir Victor would usually be found at a long table, hosting large groups of friends, with dancing troupes on their rounds of the world's best hotels and cabarets providing the entertainment. Opening nights were gala affairs, providing the Shanghai elite with

THE CATHAY PERSONALITY

The Cathay Hotel is embodied in the charming personality of a beautiful and ultra smart young woman. One would know that she bought her clothes at the best shops and knew all the right people. She knows everybody in Shanghai, of course and everybody knows her, hers is not the familiarity of the old resident. There is still something of the air of the tourist about her, definitely ensconced as she is in Shanghai's social circle.

Miss Cathay gives one the impression of being thoroughly at home all over the world and having its choicest offerings at her command. She leads a very gay life during the season and entertains lavishly. Her guests come from all over the world as well as from Shanghai's elite. Many of them do not stay long but she speeds the parting with the same good cheer with which she welcomes newcomers. Her hospitality is so extensive as to meet all tastes, whether one wishes a cup of tea or a dinner for a hundred guests. Somewhat formal in disposition she bows to the wishes of the more Bohemian of her acquaintances and maintains the Tower Night Club for them. One could hardly be said to know Shanghai without meeting Miss Cathay.

North-China Daily News, *15 February 1936*

The Cathay Hotel

an opportunity to parade their latest Paris fashions. The popularity of the Saturday night programmes reached a peak in 1934, when two immensely talented dancing couples – Caloris and Mia Monna, and Frank Alexander and Elizabeth Swanson – put on a show reportedly unsurpassed in Shanghai.

Americans Harris and Yvonne Ashburn, and the Di Gaetano dancers, made a sensational debut, with their mix of classical, tap and acrobatics, in October 1935, when Sir Victor's 100 or so guest-list read like a Who's Who of Shanghai. China's most respected diplomat, Dr. Wellington Koo, and his wife, the Countess de Courelles, together

The sultry Ganin Sisters appeared in the Cathay ballroom in 1935

Festive holiday periods and national observances were treated with a vitality and vigour seldom experienced at home. The hotel's Christmas and New Year's parties were without peer, with guests being treated to surprise 'favours' from the house of Maison Charlier of France. Henry Nathan's orchestra pumped propriety on such occasions, while familiar and popular local artists including Marty Sands, Mildred Dawn, Carol Bateman and James with representatives of Shanghai's most established families including the Ezras, Hayims and McBains, and Sassoon's friend Emily Hahn, were amongst those invited. Sassoon was rarely seen without his camera or cine-camera in hand at such events and Hahn later recounted how he liked to photograph her naked. She was also frequently seen with Sassoon at his private box at the Shanghai Race Club. Other noted performers included the exhibition dancers Souvorin and Sizikova, and the Andreef sisters.

Left *A striking and clever couple - Sizakov and Souvorin at the Cathay Hotel, 1935*

Right *Marty Sands and Mildred Dawn at Cathay ballroom, 1935*

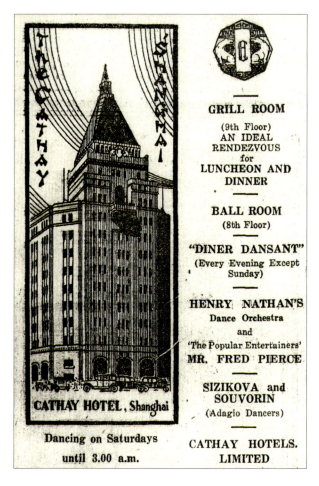
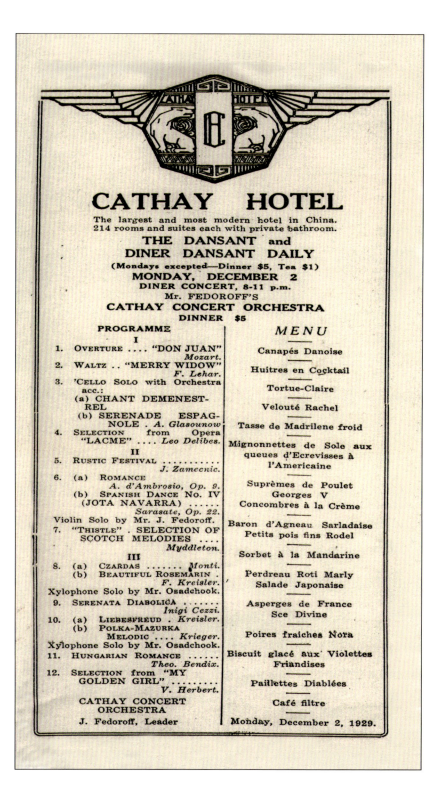

Andrew graced the dance floor with fabulously flippant displays. The ballroom, splashed with patriotic colour, was also the preferred venue for dinner dances on the occasion of Washington's Birthday.

The Cathay boasted three resident orchestras. Henry Nathan's All American Dance Orchestra accompanied the Dinner Dansant in the ballroom, while J. Ullstein's Concert Orchestra performed over lunch and during the Thé Dansant in

Wine, dine and dance. Adverts from 1932 (left) and 1929 (right)

Opposite *The Cathay Hotel was the social capital of a flamboyant city. A selection of 1930s festive adverts.*

the ground-floor lounge. Ullstein began his long and successful engagement with the Cathay Hotel in November 1929, with his classical selections counterbalancing the prevailing jazz mood. Both orchestras rested on Monday nights, when Mr. Federoff's Cathay Concert Orchestra performed a dinner concert featuring three hours of classical and romantic operatic numbers. On the note of romance, Henry Nathan struck up a relationship with one of the Worth Sisters, an American singing and dancing ensemble, while they were performing at the hotel as part of a world tour, resulting in their marriage in 1935. Sir Victor gave the bride away.

THE WORLD AND HIS WIFE

The Palace Hotel was a well-known meeting place for almost any foreigner in that area, situated as it was at the corner of the Bund Gardens and Nanking Road, with its vast lounge and plate-glass windows overlooking the street where everything was going on. It was a great attraction to office go-ers and others to partake of tea, meet their friends and generally socialise after the day's work was done. Tea and luscious cakes were served, and there was such an air of warmth and friendliness amongst all who congregated there. It was quite the thing to say to one's old friends 'Let's meet at the Palace for tea,' where one could see the world and his wife, and come across acquaintances who had just arrived back from leave, and hear the latest gossip.

Victims: All in a Lifetime,
the memoirs of Mrs. Isabelle Duck, held at the Imperial War Museum, London

1936 advert

1930 advert

EVERYTHING TO GRATIFY

The tired or lustful businessman will find here everything to gratify his desires. You can buy an electric razor, or a French dinner, or a well-cut suit. You can dance at the Tower Restaurant on the roof of the Cathay Hotel, and gossip with Freddy Kaufmann, its charming manager, about the European aristocracy or pre-Hitler Berlin. You can attend race-meetings, baseball games, football matches. You can see the latest American films. If you want girls, or boys, you can have them, at all prices, in the bath-houses and the brothels. If you want opium you can smoke it in the best company, served on a tray, like afternoon tea. Good wine is difficult to obtain in this climate, but there is enough whisky and gin to float a fleet of battleships. The jeweller and the antique-dealer await your orders, and their charges will make you imagine yourself back on Fifth Avenue or in Bond Street. Finally, if you ever repent, there are churches and chapels of all denominations.

Journey to a War,
W. H. Auden and Christopher Isherwood

The Shanghai swirl never ceased – scene at the Majestic Hotel, 1929

SHANGHAI'S RENDEZVOUS

During the 1930s the Palace Hotel Tea Lounge and Grillroom continued to be at the centre of social life for many Shanghailanders and for their visitors. The tea lounge was commonly referred to simply as 'Shanghai's Rendezvous,' while the grillroom adopted a Russian flavour with the appointment of G. Podbelsky. Formerly employed at the Astoria Hotel, St. Petersburg and the Hotel de France in Moscow, his most popular dishes included Kiev cutlets, Georgian meat orders and Russian soups.

The Palace Hotel in the early 1930s, with adverts from the same period

THE SMALL TYPHOON

The impressive figure of Dr. Anne Walter Fearn

Dr. Anne Walter Fearn was a most remarkable person. Born in Mississippi to a plantation owner and lawyer, she defied convention by studying medicine in California and Philadelphia before setting off for China to head the Soochow (Suzhou) Women's Hospital in 1893. She intended to stay just a year or two, but remained in China for most of the rest of her life.

She and her husband, Dr. John Burrus Fearn, moved to Shanghai around the turn of the twentieth century to establish a small hospital known as the Fearn Sanatorium. Operated in extravagant style, patients' meals would be served on silver trays and visitors were treated to cocktails. Fearn soon made her mark in the city. She helped establish the Shanghai American School in 1912, became president of the American's Women's Club and worked with H. H. Kung, the Nationalist Minister of Finance, on the National Child Welfare Association of China, of which he was president. On one occasion in June 1933 she hosted a large ball at the Cathay Hotel where a staggering 18,000 silver dollars was raised for the association.

Fearn's indefatigable energy and love for life earned her a reputation as the 'small typhoon.' She was best known for a rare resolve and talent in mixing people of all creeds and fancies in the multicoloured, yet partitioned, Shanghai social milieu. Before the arrival of White Russian girls during the First World War, Fearn claimed to know all the British and American residents of the bordellos in Shanghai, and after the war she made the acquaintance of many more from elsewhere. After taking up residence at the Cathay Hotel in the early 1930s she was saddened, but hardly surprised, to read an obituary of 'Singapore Kate' who had been wed at her former home just two years earlier. Fearn described her as an exquisitely beautiful girl and 'one of the most notorious harlots who trawled up and down the China Coast.' Convinced that she would soon die of heart failure, Kate married an Englishman in the hope of leading a normal life, but just couldn't forget her old profession. In the end, Fearn surmised that she died of a disease so common to the city, 'too many men, too much champagne, too much cocaine.'

In the foreword to her autobiography *My Days of Strength*, Carl Crow, famed Shanghai advertising man and author, described Fearn as 'the best-known and best-loved woman between Suez and the China Coast.' Crow believed that she achieved much more in fostering amicable relations within the foreign community, and between them and the Chinese, than many societies formed for such a purpose. Soon after she arrived in Shanghai she set about getting missionaries and businessmen, the saints and sinners, to talk to each other. Crow remarked that more often than not the prettiest girls at her parties were Chinese, 'where West met East and liked it.' Still going strong in her seventh decade, Fearn's soirées and parties at the Cathay Hotel, to which she invited all those she liked, and of those there were many, were legendary.

The high spot in her career as a social hostess was upon the visit of Mrs. Theodore Roosevelt Sr. in 1934. Representatives of every nation turned up. Among them were Mussolini's daughter, Edda, and her husband, Count Ciano; Sun Fo, the son of Sun Yat-sen; and Lord Li Ching Mai, the son of great entrepreneur and statesman Li Hung-chang (Li Hongzhang). Fearn retired in 1938 and moved to Berkeley, California, where she died just weeks before her autobiography was published in 1939.

Dr. Fearn entertains Mrs. Theodore Roosevelt and a host of glitterati in the ninth-floor lounge of the Cathay Hotel, 1934

11 CHAMPAGNE, CURFEWS AND CONFLICTS

IN SETTLED TIMES the Cathay Hotel played a genteel host, while in times of strife, and of those there were many, she acquired a new urgency and exuberance in safeguarding the social obligations of her guests. The first major call on her extended hospitality was made in the early months of 1932, when Shanghai was subverted to a state of siege as fierce fighting erupted between Japanese and Chinese troops in the Chapei (Zhabei) district of the Greater Shanghai Municipality, perilously close to the hotel. Stanley Jackson, a Sassoon family biographer, tells of an incident whilst Sassoon was lunching at the hotel, when a mine exploded 50 yards away in the river, causing the building to sway. No damage seemed to have been done and Sassoon could not find as much as a crack when he did a round of inspection. On another occasion Sassoon ventured out from what he described as 'the front row of the stalls' to film the action and narrowly escaped with his life, as a Chinese soldier, mistaking him for a sniper, fired a shot that whizzed over his head and shattered a nearby window.

Hedonism developed as an essential accessory to war and parties rolled through the night in the Cathay Ballroom following the imposition of a curfew from ten in the evening till four in the morning. Sassoon was reported to have treated his guests with magnums of pink champagne in the hotel's restaurants and bars whilst the explosive effervescence of battle was the order of the day. Following the conflict, with an armistice signed on 5 May, the battlefields of Chapei were a must-see on the hasty agenda of whirling round-the-world tourists, who were turning up on Shanghai's doorstep in ever-increasing numbers.

In early 1937 Shanghai was playing host to record numbers of tourists. Those numbers swelled in July, as many hundreds, who had been caught up in fighting around Peking (Beijing), were 'packed like sardines' on special trains headed for the presumed safety of Shanghai. Peking fell

Opposite *The Union Jack flies high on the Cathay Hotel (left) and many other buildings along the Bund, 1934*

135

to the Japanese that month, marking the advent of the Sino-Japanese War. Shanghai was placed under an unofficial state of emergency, but still wore its impervious social armour. Although Shanghailanders had witnessed a number of minor skirmishes around the city in early August they went about their business and social routines as normal, resting faith in the sanctity of the International Settlement and a belief that the fighting would be restricted to the surrounding Chinese controlled areas. As for Shanghai's visitors, a columnist for the *North-China Daily News* surmised that they, in some bizarre sense, were entertained by the new siege conditions – 'the tourist who is not as used to wars as the old resident has proved a very good sport about accepting the annoyances inherent in the situation. She wishes that she might have seen Peking, not to mention Korea and Manchuria, but she is kind enough to say that she is glad to have had more time to spend in Shanghai.'

However, by the time that newspaper report was printed on 15 August, nobody was glad to be in the city. On 14 August, two bombs fell on the corner of Nanking Road and the Bund, damaging both the Cathay Hotel and the Palace Hotel, and inflicting death and mutilation on hundreds of innocent victims. Sassoon heard the news of what was to become known as 'Bloody Saturday,' while in far away Bombay, where he was tending to his racing establishment.

Both hotels soon recovered from their superficial tears and wounds and they, like the majority of businesses in Shanghai, put on a brave face, announcing business as usual just five weeks later on 18 September. However, the Cathay Ballroom was still out of operation and the Palace Hotel's gashing wounds on its uppermost floor were only partly sealed by matting. Ullstein's orchestra, in harmony with the melancholy mood of Shanghai society, played just two short performances at lunch and tea-time in the ground floor lounge, which, like the adjoining Cathay Bar, closed at nine in the evening. Freddy Kaufmann, manager of

Indian policeman, employed by the Shanghai Municipal Police, were a common site on the Bund. The Cathay Hotel and the Palace Hotel can be seen to the right.

Opposite *Beyond imagination - scenes of tragedy outside the Palace Hotel, 14 August 1937*

BLOODY SATURDAY

On the morning of 14 August, the Chinese, for the first time, began bombing attacks from the air. Their target was the Japanese flagship *Idzumo*, moored near the Japanese Consulate, some 400 yards away from the Cathay Hotel. The initial bombardment caused a panic stricken flight of people from the Hongkew (Hongkou) district, where many bombs had fallen, to the Bund and its neighbouring streets. In the Peking Room on the eighth floor of the Cathay Hotel, the 'front row of the stalls,' Mrs. Theodore Roosevelt, Jr. and her son Quentin watched on as plumes of grey smoke coalesced into the greyness of the day. Mrs. Roosevelt described the Bund with its seething mass of refugees, many clutching their meagre belongings, as comparable to 'Cooney Island Beach on the Fourth of July.' But this was no fun fair, and fear set in as she watched a huge crowd of Chinese chase a small number of Japanese, one of whom she witnessed being stabbed and brutally beaten. Soon after, when the anti-aircraft guns on the *Idzumo* broke loose, Louis Suter, the Cathay Hotel manager, decided that it was time for them to leave.

Just minutes after the Roosevelt's had departed, two misdirected bombs from Chinese aircraft whistled and whirled down from the skies.

One bomb, weighing over 250 pounds, punctured the roof of the Palace Hotel, setting it ablaze, destroying the fifth-floor dining rooms and killing many Chinese staff in their quarters. It blew away half the roof and floor at the point of impact, and fragments pierced the heart of the hotel right down to its second floor. Another bomb had glanced off the side of the neighbouring Cathay Hotel, damaging a seventh-floor room before exploding in the street below, stirring glass and steel into a deadly storm.

From the hotels' doorways and windows, people gazed forth dumbly, shocked to the very core of their beings by the instant annihilation. Shapeless heaps of those sheltering from the attack lay piled in their main entrances and doorways. Many stricken were found deep inside the Sassoon House Arcade, blown there by the great concussion that had smashed all its shop windows to smithereens.

Death and destruction on the door of the Cathay Hotel (including photo on opposite page)

It was 4.27 p.m. The Cathay Hotel's clock froze as the bombs hit.

TIME magazine recounted the experience of United Pressman John R. Morris, who was in the Palace Hotel lobby when the bombs fell:

I ran out to the Nanking Road side of the narrow lounge, hurdling overturned tea tables, chairs and prostrate forms of guests seeking the safety of the floor. Through the gaping windows on the Nanking Road I could see at least 50 persons writhing on the sidewalk and roadway. Three foreigners were trying to crawl over the bodies of dead Chinese . . . out on the street I saw a white woman crouched in the middle of Nanking Road, assisting her daughter in giving birth to a child, while a hail of death pelted from the skies.

Less fortunate was Robert Karl Reischauer, a Princeton University lecturer acting as a tour guide for the summer, who died in hospital after receiving a leg injury in the blast. Only that morning Reischauer had moved from the Astor House Hotel, close to where the *Idzumo* was moored, to the Palace Hotel, believing that he would be safer there. TIME reported that death came too for an American barmaid known to Shanghai simply as Dodo Dynamite.

The casualties, both foreign and Chinese, numbered over 400 with around 150 fatalities. The toll would have been much higher had it not been a Saturday afternoon, with many of the nearby shops already closed. Chinese authorities reported that the missiles were released onto their unintended targets as the planes' bomb racks had been damaged by Japanese fire. Some speculate that the 'accident' had been ruthlessly contrived in order, among other reasons, to draw international attention to the conflict.

'Bloody Saturday,' as 14 August had been dubbed, was a day Shanghai never recovered from.

The siege of the city lasted until November, whereupon the Japanese occupied the Chinese city and districts to the north of the International Settlement. In early December, following Chiang Kai-shek's withdrawal from Shanghai, the Japanese marched through the International Settlement in a victory parade. The incident marked the beginning of a spiralling downturn in the fortunes of the city, as the economy faltered, inflation propelled prices beyond people's means and the Japanese assumed increasing influence. Foreign trade on the Yangtze River, Shanghai's principal raison d'être, had been driven away and the great port city languished in idleness and fear.

Top Left *Three observation planes from the Japanese Air Fleet fly high over the Cathay Hotel, February 1932*

Top Right *Debonair Freddy Kaufmann*

Bottom *Soon back in the swing of things, advert from late 1938*

the Tower Night Club, was eager to get things back into full swing and within a month Ullstein was playing there over dinner. Eric de Reyner, a singer with a boyish grin, nicknamed the 'whispering pianist,' then performed until the doors shut at 11 p.m. The ballroom was back in action by the middle of November.

Over the following winter the Cathay Ballroom and the Tower Night Club, like dancing partners, took turns hosting Shanghai's pleasure seekers. At the Tower, with tables in heavy demand, French chef Gabriel Comte personally supervised dinners accompanied by romantic jazz by pianist Waldy with Gene Kirkor on drums. In the ballroom, the all-American Syd's Cathay Syncopaters played fox-trots,

blues and waltzes each Saturday until midnight.

The following summer season witnessed the Cathay's nightspots in an unfamiliarly restful mood, as they remained closed. The ballroom, which had remained open just one night a week, closed completely in May, in anticipation that the Tower Night Club would continue as the centre of entertainment, but it, too, closed a month later. For many foreigners who had not left Shanghai, it was a time for a tightening of belts as inflation hit the roof, turmoil hit the money markets and terrorism hit the streets. On 10 June a period of fragile calm was broken, when the most unwanted of guests, death, arrived on the Cathay Hotel's doorstep. Just before noon, a barrage of gunfire sang out, as would-be assassins set their sights on Mr. Yu Chueh-sen stepping out of Sassoon House on Jinkee (Dianchi) Road. Mr. Yu, a businessman and vice-chairman of the Japanese sponsored Chinese Civic Association, was hit in the neck and shoulder. Passers-by scuttled for cover as heavy crossfire erupted between police, Mr. Yu's bodyguards and the assailants, shattering windows in the hotel and splashing blood on its granite face. When silence fell, J. Karpoff, one of Mr. Yu's bodyguards, was found dead at the entrance to the hotel. Christopher Isherwood and W. H. Auden, who were heading to the hotel for a cup of coffee as the bullets flared, noticed a small crowd gazing at a fresh pool of blood upon their arrival. Hearing that Mr. Yu had survived the attack, they surmised that 'next time, most probably, he won't escape alive.'

Shanghai was peppered with numerous

Top *A member of the Shanghai Municipal Police apprehends one of Mr. Yu Cheuh-sen's attackers*

Bottom *Crowds gather around the car used by Mr. Yu Cheuh-sen*

141

The three faces of the Tower, 1936 adverts

ing on the wall of the Yokohama Specie Bank on the Bund and another in the compound of the Shanghai Land Investment Company on Jinkee (Dianchi) Road, near Sassoon House. Just before lunch on 3 August a grenade exploded in the Palace Hotel's backyard. Fortunately, few of the usually large crowd of regular diners had arrived and no one was seriously injured. The reopening of the Tower Night Club at the Cathay Hotel in September gave some assurance that the summer of discontent

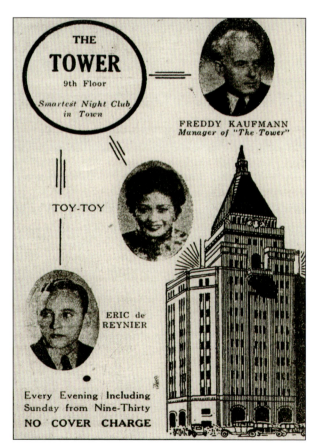

bombing and shooting incidents that coming summer. On 12 June, five hand grenades were thrown at targets in the heart of the International Settlement, though no loss of life was recorded. The violence escalated on 7 July – the first anniversary of the 'Marco Polo Bridge' incident south of Peking that sparked the national war of resistance against Japan – when the city crackled with bombs, hand grenades and gunfire. Fatal incidents occurred close to the Cathay Hotel, with two bombs explod-

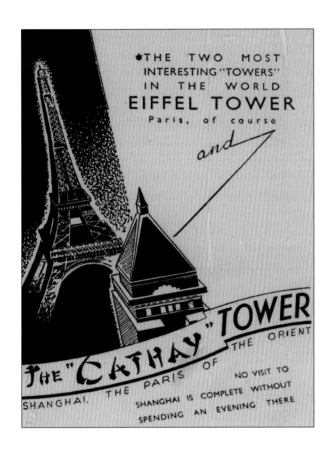

missal of Alfred Gottlieb, its Hungarian manager. Gottlieb, a Jewish refugee who had escaped the Nazi menace in Europe less than a year earlier, had been overcharging guests for drinks and cigarettes. The Shanghai Municipal Police discovered a substantial stash of such booty in room 626, where he resided. Regarding it as a foolish act of someone living in difficult circumstances, Sassoon decided not to bring criminal charges against him. More than likely, Gottlieb was one of the many thousands of beneficiaries of Sassoon's enormous generosity in establishing schemes to settle and rehabilitate Jews who been deprived of their existence in Europe. The Kadoorie family, majority shareholders in The Hongkong and Shanghai Hotels, was drawing to a close.

A new mood of optimism greeted the New Year in 1939. The Palace Hotel underwent extensive repairs and improvements to all its bedrooms and public areas, and the top floor dining room that had been destroyed on 'Bloody Saturday' was converted into 13 extra rooms. At the Cathay Hotel, the Tower Night Club was back in full swing and a new eighth-floor nightspot, called the Pelican, opened in March. However, the new club's career only lasted until November, coincident with the dis-

Top *Two cities, two towers - 1938 advert*

Bottom *The Tower, Shanghai's long established night club, finds a new playmate in 1939*

Limited, who owned the Palace Hotel, also made huge contributions to the welfare of some 18,000 Jewish refugees who landed on Shanghai's doorstep.

As the storm clouds of war gathered over Europe, the Cathay Hotel played host to numerous unexpected guests, including various military and diplomatic associations. Spies and informers, agents and double-agents became part of the furniture. Storms of the natural kind also hit Shanghai in July 1939, when two passers-by were electrocuted by a falling wire outside the hotel.

Sassoon displayed a solemn outward courtesy towards his Japanese visitors, and their military officers were treated with scrupulous politeness when they dined at the hotel. However, in the public arena, he was outspoken in his support of Chiang Kai-shek and the Nationalist Party, and adamant in the belief that Japan would be defeated in China.

Sassoon personally donated £20,000 to the British War Fund that had been created following the outbreak of the Second World War. With a love of flying and his past record of service in the Royal Naval Air Service in the First World War, Sassoon took over as president of the Royal Air Force Association Club in 1939. He hosted numerous 'patriotic lunches' to raise funds

Patriotism a long way from home, adverts from early 1941 (including image from opposite page)

for the war effort in the club's palatial premises in the dome atop the Hongkong and Shanghai Bank building on the Bund. Stanley Jackson recounts that, soon after war was declared, Sassoon 'sold two valuable sapphires and a number of jade necklaces in America and gave the proceeds to the R.A.F. for the purchase of fighter aircraft.' He also tells of Sassoon's response to a question by a humiliated Japanese officer, who had been out-gunned in his own game of subterfuge during dinner at the Cathay Hotel. When asked why he was so anti-Japanese, Sassoon replied, 'I am not anti-Japanese at all, I am simply pro-Sassoon and very pro-British.'

The Cathay Hotel took the lead in bowing to a call for more responsibility and sense in a city where elaborate entertainment was viewed either as a necessary indulgence, or as a drain on the British war effort. Following a month's closure in June 1940, the Tower Night Club reopened with the management doing its best to 'infuse a ray of cheer into these gloomy days' by announcing that all profits would be given to the war fund. They proved that, despite demands for quiet living, lavish entertainment could still add around 4,000 Chinese Dollars to the coffers of the British govern-

145

Sir Victor Sasson (centre), with Henry Morriss of the North-China Daily News to his left, in the Tower Night Club, 1939

ment each month.

However, there were gloomy days ahead for the Cathay Hotels, Limited. It was plagued by two major strikes in 1941. On the evening of 12 April the entire Cathay Hotel staff walked out in sympathy with their counterparts at the Cathay Mansions, where two lift operators had been dismissed. Calls from the staff for their reinstatement, and a 100 percent pay rise to boot, were ignored by the management, who pointed out that they were already 40 percent better paid than those staff in other hotels. In total, 1,000 Cathay Hotels, Limited employees left their duties. The management, adamant not to let the workers have their way, were not unduly concerned by the walkout, which they saw as an opportunity to solve overstaffing problems and rid themselves of 'troublemakers.'

In an attempt to fill the gap, a few servants were hired from the vast army of foreign unemployed in the city. However, service in the bar, restaurant and Tower Night Club came to a complete standstill, with guests being forced to go elsewhere. While many guests were beginning to grumble, the workers were slandering management by suggesting that they were more concerned with their horse racing than with settling their grievances. The solution lay in the hands of Mr. Jean George Lipsman, who was appointed as general manager of the Cathay Hotels, Limited during the strike. He refused to increase wages and informed the strikers that their positions would be taken by Russian and Jewish refugees if they didn't see reason.

A second, more severe, strike hit on 18 August. This strike, allegedly initiated by a Nanking-sponsored labour union, was not as spontaneous as the earlier one. The direct cause was the arrest of 20 radical members of the Shanghai Municipality Foreign Hotels Chinese Employees Mutual Aid Society by French Police. Despite fears over physical reprisals, almost all of Sassoon's 2,500 Chinese employees walked out in support. A few clerks stood to duty at the Cathay Hotel, where only the Tower Night Club remained open for liquid refreshment.

The management, yet again, threatened to hire a complete staff of European workers if there was no early appeasement. Tensions and grievances were high, and Settlement police were called in to protect the hotel and its foreign staff, some of whom had been sent letters containing bullets. The management took the brazen step of announcing the end of the strike two days later, when it hired 100 German-Jewish refugees to replace the kitchen and dining room staff. They intended to keep

Members of the American Junior Chamber of Commerce step away from economic strife and warfare at their dinner dance in the Cathay Ballroom, 1939

on such foreign workers after the situation had been fully resolved, since they were actually cheaper to employ than the local Chinese. Most of the room boys scurried back to work when they realised that the management was in earnest. However, the majority of Chinese staff who remained on strike were given a blunt ultimatum: 'return to work within two days or never return again!' Some returned – some didn't.

Meanwhile, protests were hurled at the management over the poor quality of service from the new occidental staff, with many guests walking out in disgust. The stalemate continued until 4 September, when the workers finally agreed to management terms. The new conditions, designed to put an end to political agitation amongst staff, gave them the right to dismiss or transfer any employee. However, a good service bonus was instituted for those staff who had completed a certain number of years service and paid sick leave was promised. The German-Jewish refugees, Russians and Portuguese, hired during the strike, were summarily discharged following the Chinese employees return. Few were to benefit from the new system, though, as an event that would change the course of the Second World War and pervert Shanghai's celebrated past into an indefinite future lay in waiting. Even in July 1941, Sassoon, quoted in *Israel's Messenger* (courtesy of Maisie J. Meyer), still believed that there would be no war in the Pacific 'because Japan realises the futility of attacking the United States, and contrary to propagandists has no intention to dominate the world. A war between the two is not even a remote possibility today.'

It remained a remote possibility for most Shanghailanders right up until the day of Pearl Harbour. But come that day, 8 December 1941 in the East, the era of British rule in Shanghai came to an end in flash of gunfire, as the British gunboat *Peterel*, shelled and ablaze, sank into the disturbed depths of the Whangpoo (Huangpu) River. By the end of the day Japanese forces had control of all foreign businesses and institutions in the International Settlement.

Fortunately, Sir Victor Sassoon was again in Bombay on the day his empire fell to the Japanese. He had left Shanghai the previous spring on the advice of Lucien Ovadia, his cousin and business mentor. Ovadia, who had worked at the E. D. Sassoon offices in Manchester before coming to Shanghai in 1933, was also very lucky as result, in the words of Stanley Jackson, of 'a happy accident.' During that year, Ovadia had been in negotiations with the American Consulate, which was eager to purchase the Metropole Hotel. They insisted that the final arrangements for the sale should be made in London and Ovadia duly set sail. He arrived in London only to learn that the deal had fallen through and heard the news before reaching Shanghai on his return trip. Ovadia settled in New York, from where he managed to transfer a mass of the company's frozen assets from Shanghai and Hong Kong.

Those not so fortunate woke up to a strange new day at the office. Shanghai-born Rena Krasno recalls, in her book *Strangers Always, a Jewish Family in Wartime Shanghai,* a friend who, upon hearing the news of Japanese invasion, rushed to work at the Sassoon offices in Sassoon House in an attempt to destroy company files. 'A group of Japanese Blue Jackets marched in and ordered [the employees] to stop and go about their normal routine. That went on for a while before the Japanese who belonged to the *Idzumo Maru* landing party took over the business completely.'

A brace of Japanese sentries guarded the hotels' entrances. All British consular officials and staff were swiftly moved to the Cathay Hotel, while their American counterparts, ironically, were moved to the Metropole Hotel, opposite their former offices. Over the following days all enemy nationals aged over 14, numbering some

Head on with the new Japanese administration - more than 50 Britons and Americans gather at the Metropole Hotel on 11 December. Lt. A. Matsuda (centre) presides

10,000, the majority British, were forced to register at the Japanese Military Liaison Office in Hamilton House. 'Failure to register will bring about severe punishment,' the authorities warned.

On 11 December some influential members of the British and American communities were invited to a meeting, described by the Japanese as an 'informal' gathering, at the Metropole Hotel. Presided over by Lieutenant Matsuda, under specific instructions from the High Command of the Japanese Imperial Army and Navy, its alleged purpose was to discover more about the 'desires, hopes, difficulties and impressions of the local Britons and Americans that have arisen in the wake of the Japanese occupation.' Over 50 people attended and the *Shanghai Sunday Times*, now a Japanese propaganda machine, reported that they 'thanked' the Japanese forces for their orderly and courteous conduct. The Japanese authorities hoped that nothing would mar their 'friendly understanding' reminding those assembled that they had not been thrown into concentration camps, as many might have expected.

The politeness and solemnity of the occasion was broken by uproarious laughter when J. B. Powell, celebrated American editor of the *China Weekly Review*, was asked, 'what did you expect the Japanese

John B. Powell

forces to do to you when they entered the Settlement?' He retorted, 'I did not expect anything worse than being shot.'

Lieutenant Matsuda presided over another meeting at the Metropole Hotel, attended by around 250 British and Americans, on 22 December. He gave his assurance that the Japanese held no animosity or personal ill feelings towards any of the audience, adding that those engaging in subversive activities would not 'deserve any sympathy.' Mr Harry Arnhold, of Sassoon's associate company, was in attendance.

There was one notable absentee from that meeting: J. B. Powell. A real fighter for China's cause, he had already been plucked from his room at the Metropole Hotel and dumped at Bridge House, headquarters of the Japanese Kempeitai (military police), where he was subjected to torture of the cruellest kind. Powell was in a very poor condition when he was repatriated and both his feet were amputated on the journey back home. Harry Arnhold also endured a spell at Bridge House, and surely the same fate would have fallen upon Sir Victor Sassoon had he been in range.

Those diplomats living at the Cathay or Metropole hotels continued to receive their salaries, enabling them to maintain a reasonable standard of living and they were free to move around the old Settlement area as they wished. In early February 1942, around 130 American, British and Dutch consular representatives and their families were moved to four floors of the Cathay Mansions. Most were repatriated by August that year. On 1 March 1942 the *Shanghai Sunday Times* announced that all the former Cathay Hotels, Limited, properties had reopened for 'business as usual.' But behind the desks sat Japanese managers. The Cathay Hotel was under the management of Mr. S. Takahashi, possibly in the employ of the Japanese Embassy, and Mr. S. Matsuzaki managed the Metropole Hotel. Mr. M. Kanaya assumed management of the Palace Hotel, while its former Swiss manager, Mr. A. Matti, continued serve as his number two.

Parts of the Cathay Hotel had been converted into spacious godowns (warehouses) and a large number of rooms were rear-

The second larger meeting, held at the Metropole Hotel on 22 December

ranged in Japanese style, while the Japanese Army's Press Bureau had commandeered parts of the Metropole Hotel. Though few records survive of how the businesses fared, it is certain that many of those in need of simple accommodation were unable to find it. On one night alone in November 1942, 517 beggars froze to death on the streets of the city. In January 1944, Domei, a Japanese news agency, reported that the Cathay and Metropole hotels had been transferred from Japanese control to that of the puppet Chinese National Government, though they were still providing capital and 'managerial assistance.' Whoever was actually in control didn't matter to those interred in detention camps around the city, many of whom were fighting for survival and looking forward to the day when they could again find freedom and liberty.

12 | STRANGERS IN SHANGHAI

When the Cathay Hotels, Limited resumed control of its properties in late 1945, its representatives returned to an alien city, a city of torment, a city of chaos and a city hanging on to life by a slender thread. Old Shanghailanders looked back on the pre-war days and reminisced that the city was never as bad as it was painted. The Shanghai Municipal Council and the lines of the International Settlement had vanished forever. Even traffic, which had previously kept to the left, was forced to change allegiance, as a matter of expediency, to the right-hand side of the road. The new Shanghai Council, with its novice officials, took over the running of the new Shanghai – an overworked city, now of some four and a half million residents. The British played little or no part in the city that, just a decade earlier, they had considered their own.

J. G. Lipsman's main task, upon resuming his duties as head of the Cathay Hotels, Limited, was to right the considerable damage caused to all of its properties. Cathay Mansions and the Metropole Hotel had been converted into 'fortresses' and munitions factories with machine gun nests installed. In early 1945, the entire Cathay Estate was taken over by Japanese troops for their headquarters, and air raid shelters and anti-aircraft gun positions became part of the new landscape. At the Cathay Hotel, roughly half of the 240 rooms had been redecorated by early December 1945 and the ninth-floor grill-room was only able to offer modest snacks for lunch. The company was also eager to put things right with those staff that had quit under Japanese management. Fred Marcus, a post-war employee of the company, revealed in his memoir *Survival in*

The task of rehabilitating the Cathay Hotel's interests were in the capable hands of Mr. J. G. Lipsman

Opposite *Post-war scene outside the Metropole Hotel*

Gen. Marshall with Nationalist party dignitaries at the Cathay Hotel, December 1945

Shanghai that lost salaries were paid in full. The cost of putting everything back in order came at a high price, and hotel rates were many times their pre-war levels. Sir Victor's cousin, Lucien Ovadia, returned as chairman of the Sassoon interests just in time to add the finishing touches to the 1945 Christmas celebrations.

High-ranking American and British officers and embassy staff occupied many of the Cathay Hotel's rooms. In October General George E. Stratemeyer, standing in as Acting Commander of the US Forces in China for General Wedemeyer, moved in. On his return in November, Wedemeyer took over Sir Victor Sassoon's personal suite before it was passed on to General George C. Marshall, who arrived on 20 December. Marshall, the former US Army Chief of Staff, was on a mission that ultimately failed, to mediate between Nationalist and Communist forces. Nationalist officials hosted parties for the Americans in the hotel to celebrate the camaraderie between the two nations. Later, Claire Chennault, the former leader of the illustrious 'Flying Tigers,' stayed there. Meanwhile, many US Armed Forces were put up at the Metropole Hotel, under the management of Mr. O. Stahly, and the Chinese 94th Army had been billeted at Cathay Mansions, managed by Mr. E. Negri, in September. The top two floors of the Palace Hotel were taken over by the US Navy, who stayed until October 1946. Leo Gaddi, who later found fame as the manager of Hong Kong's Peninsula hotel, presided over the property.

In early 1946 the newly refurbished Tower Night Club tried to exclude the military rank and file by restricting entry to those wearing evening dress on three nights each week, but later capitulated and made it Friday nights only 'by special request of our patrons who are not in possession of evening dress due to the abnormal circumstances.' Evening suits were the last things on the minds of the hordes of American naval personnel on shore leave, in what was seen as one of the best liberty ports in the Orient. However, Philip Chu, who had reopened his shop in the Sassoon House Arcade – selling oriental rugs, jewellery, ivory, jade, curios and furniture – was doing a roaring trade.

The three Cathay Hotels, Limited properties were soon back on their feet. Helene de Groot, columnist for *The Enquirer and News* in Michigan, wrote that:

> their elaborate dining rooms glitter with sparkling crystal, silver, and important persons. The maitre d'hotel and the dignified waiters almost overwhelm you with their old world gallantry, courtesy, and flawless service. Musicians serenade you with soothing dinner music. Food is served in a number of elaborate courses and when the diner picks up his check, he finds its total a fairly reasonable amount, and certainly worth the superb service.

Yet these were not normal times. The financial and commodity markets were once again at a heightened frenzy, and Communist forces were making significant advances in China's heartland. Whilst Shanghai's businessmen strove to protect their vanishing fortunes, millions of others just fought to survive. A new body under the umbrella of the United Nations, an Economic Commission for Asia and the Far East (UNECAFE), was established to help the economic reconstruction of the region, with its first formal meeting taking place in the Cathay Hotel Ballroom in June 1947. After the ten-day conference representatives from the UK, France, China,

Netherlands, Australia, Philippines, India and Siam (Thailand) came up with an initial strategy to help the homeless and destitute, despite an objection by the Russian delegation.

After some six years of residing in Bombay, with occasional visits to England, Sir Victor Sassoon made his first visit back to Shanghai in December 1947 to rid himself of some of the 'too many interests' that he held in the city. He was only to make one further visit to Shanghai, in April 1948. On that occasion he spoke to the Rotary Club at the Metropole Hotel on the subject of Russia and the world. Sassoon's prediction that there would be no third world war between the US and

Delegates at the first Unecafe meeting

155

Russia using nuclear weapons was one that would stand the test of time. He told the club 'I hate Russia's ideology. I hate her nullification of freedom, but I have the greatest admiration for her people and for her leader.'

The uncertainty of the times also prompted The Hongkong and Shanghai Hotels, Limited to accept an offer for the purchase of the Palace Hotel by millionaire tycoon Teng Chung-ho in 1947. There was a rumour, reported in the *China Daily Tribune*, that the hotel was to be demolished and replaced by a new 18-storey bank and office building. Yet, as in times of uncertainty in the past, when its previous owners had wished it replaced by a more modern structure, it was not to be. Tug Wilson, the Cathay Hotel's architect, remarked in 1930 that the Palace Hotel was 'never a thing of beauty,' and 'it is hoped that it will soon give way to something better.' That it didn't had much to do with yet another turn in the topsy-turvy fortunes of the greying Asian metropolis.

In 1948 rates at the Palace Hotel and Cathay Hotel spiralled upwards with the fury of a typhoon. Inflation became so rampant that on the habitual morning visit to the bank, bundles of notes changed hands without question of the amount being correct. Nobody cared to count and taxi drivers, amongst others, faithfully pocketed the neatly tied stashes of paper. Diners at the hotels' restaurants would pay by cheque, but often lump in a valise stuffed with paper cash as a tip. In August 1948 Leslie Haylen, an Australian Labour MP and a successful playwright and novelist writing under the pen-name Sutton Woodfield, stayed at the Cathay Hotel, in a room as big as 'Central Railway Station with a bed out of a Hollywood film.' He recounted:

The big day arrives, the Tower Night Club is back in business

a coolie crouched by my door, and there was a room-boy, drinks waiter, and a dry-cleaner and laundry-man at the end of my buzzer ... luxury! I had lunch in the restaurant, overwhelmed with service, and paid one million gold yuan (in paper) for a bottle of very indifferent wine. A gentleman at my table was reading in an early edition of the afternoon paper what money was worth at noon – an hour before. He would get another edition at 3.30 p.m. to see if he could still afford to eat. That was normal for 1948, but there was something else. I was told this hotel had been built on opium. I felt drugged all the time I stayed there.

In October that year Henry McLemore of the *Los Angeles Times* stayed in the Cathay Suite, which he swore 'was just about the same size as the playing surface of the Yale Bowl and the charge was evidently by the square foot. Had we stayed there a week I would have to take up rickshaw pulling as a sideline.' Hotel rates were hiked by over 1,000 percent between August and November!

Except in times of conflict and crisis, Shanghai didn't figure largely in the diet of the leading American newspapers. Lots of hastily concocted stories had been served up during the events of 1937 and the Communist advance on Shanghai in May 1949 whisked up another round of sensationalism. On 2 May 1949 the *Los Angeles Times* reported that the Palace Hotel, Cathay Hotel, Grosvenor House and Cathay Mansions had each been taken over by around 100 Nationalist troops, setting up gun placements in windows and on their roofs.

George Vine, assistant editor at the *North-China Daily News*, in conversation with Noel Barber, recounted the scene when an officer, followed by 50 troops walked into the Cathay Hotel and politely, but firmly,

Mr. Leslie Haylen

and other wall decorations. 'Soon only the gilded Buddhas, smiling in their niches remained,' Vine recalled. The troops set up their base in the club, where they installed a huge rice-cooking pot and reportedly threw banana skins from its balcony to the gawping masses below.

Shanghai was suddenly, yet again, shrouded under curfew. It was lights out at nine in the evening. The Palace Hotel announced, 'that on the orders of the garrison commander, he had come to requisition a dozen rooms to install machine-gun posts overlooking the waterfront and other vital points.' Vine heard one soldier ask innocently, 'Where can we billet our mules?' Guests were hurriedly moved to other hotels while the staff rescued the best furniture, mainly from the Tower Night Club. They wheeled out a grand piano, removed rugs, furniture and liquor, and pulled down hand-carved dragons, silk lanterns

Something to celebrate in uncertain times. The staff of AAU (today's AIA) on the roof of their offices with the Cathay Hotel in the background

The bronze winged angel that perched atop the landmark War Memorial on the Bund disappeared during the Japanese occupation of Shanghai. (See photo on opposite page) Remembrance services were still held there after 1945.

resorted to hiring a troupe of hula dancers and a new swing band to perform from 2.00 p.m. till 6.00 p.m. The party came to an abrupt end on 27 May, when after a couple of days of fierce fighting, Communist forces marched triumphantly along Shanghai's famed waterfront.

The *China Weekly Review* told the story of the arrival of People's Liberation Army (PLA) at the Palace Hotel. The commander of the several hundred troops first asked if they could be given rooms at half price. The manager agreed to this. Then the PLA officer explained that the soldiers were not used to such luxurious surroundings and asked if it would be too much trouble to remove the furniture from the rooms. Finally, the troop commander said that perhaps some of the hotel's permanent guests, particularly foreigners, might be upset to see a lot of soldiers coming in and out and asked whether arrangements could be made for his men to use the back door! The *Review* reported that 'the persons working in the hotel say you would never know the soldiers were living there.' The quiet, Communist revolutionaries closed the door on Nationalist Party rule in China that had been celebrated in the very same building on 29 December 1911, when Dr. Sun Yat-sen entertained over one hundred of his boisterous revolutionary

followers after his election as President of the Republic of China.

Most of the Cathay Hotel's guests had already left by early May and in August the *New York Times* reported that, despite cheaper rates, it had 'become a grey and gloomy monolith.' By that time all remaining guests had been shifted to the Metropole Hotel, 'where servants still outnumbered guests by over forty to one.' That ratio became even greater following the founding of the People's Republic of China on 1 October 1949. Lucien Ovadia was now charged with footing the bill

159

for some 1,400 largely redundant Cathay Hotels, Limited staff, whose employment rights were protected by the new regime. At what turned out to be the last meeting of the Cathay Hotels, Limited at Holland House in Hong Kong on 27 December 1950, it was reported that, 'the company had remained dormant during the year and there was no development.' Tax bills mounted up and in June 1951 a deal was made allowing the leasing of the hotel to the Chinese government in exchange for payment. The Cathay Hotels, Limited disappeared from the Hong Kong Companies Register on 3 August 1951, at which time its directors, apart from Ovadia, included Thomas Douglas Drysdale and Henry Rennie Cleland. Lucien Ovadia was eventually repatriated in June 1952.

Opposite *Victorious PLA troops outside the Cathay and Palace Hotels, 1949*

Picture perfect. The Peace Hotel, 1950s

Tunisian visitors enjoying themselves in the ballroom, October 1957

In the 1950s and 1960s the Peace Hotel received guests from the Soviet Bloc, and friendship groups from other Asian and European countries. They could hardly be described as tourists. They were a select band of invited writers and artists, sinologists, sports men and women, politicians and trade unionists. Visitors were treated as honoured guests, heaped upon with official hospitality and shown every courtesy. Although the billiard tables were back in action and the hotel shop

National Day celebrations on the Bund, 1954

The former Cathay Mansions in a new guise as the Jin Jiang Hotel, 1950s

was stocked with fine arts and crafts at low 'friendship' prices, very little in the way of entertainment was offered. Obligatory receptions and meetings, alongside outings to acrobatic shows, operatic performances and kindergarten visits, were strictly supervised by Chinese host organisations. The China International Travel Service (C.I.T.S.), China's own 'Intourist,' was established in 1956 to take care of all aspects of foreign travel in China. However, the hotel was rarely more than half full and ordinary Chinese citizens were refused entry.

China was proud to show off her achievements under Communism and to promote her position in the world. The Peace Hotel and the former Cathay Mansions were the only hotels in Shanghai permitted to receive foreign envoys. Sassoon's sister hotels were back in business again – but this time around, they operated on a model of friendship rather than financial gain. Profit was thought of in cultural terms. Cathay Mansions now operated as the Jin Jiang (Beautiful River) Hotel, but was known to many as the 'King Kong' – the name of a Shanghai restaurant and a common form of reference reserved for foreigners. Of Sassoon's other former interests, the Metropole Hotel continued to play host to Chinese guests, under the guise of the Xincheng (New City) Hotel; while the neighbouring

Vintage luggage tag

165

THERE'S A TAVERN IN THE TOWN

Back in the 1930s Henry Nathan's All American Dance Orchestra, the Cathay Hotel's resident jazz ensemble, was renowned for its rendition of 'There's a Tavern in the Town.' Whilst the toe-tapping, sing-along classic was not in the Old Peace Hotel Jazz Band's repertoire when they were formed in 1980, they too were to find renown for performing in the most famous tavern in the town at the Peace Hotel. Breaking the solitude of the night in a city that had been deprived of nightly entertainment for almost a generation, the Peace Hotel Jazz Band, as they were later known, despite their advancing in years, were soon playing their own inimitable brand of pre-War swing to the rapturous applause of audiences from around the globe. Jimmy Carter, Ronald Reagan and Queen Elizabeth II were among those visiting dignitaries treated to a night out, Old Shanghai style, in the hotel's historic granite-clad bar. The average of age of the six-piece ensemble was 66 in 1989 and some of them, including their leader, Mr. Zhou Wanrong, were still performing until the Jazz Bar closed its doors, to a rendition of their signature tune, Auld Lang Syne, in 2007.

Top *Henry Nathan's Orchestra, 1932. 'There's a Tavern in the Town' was one of the quintette's favourite numbers*

Bottom *The Cathay Hotel bar, 1933*

Top *Swinging in the new era, the jazz band performs in the lobby, 1978*

Bottom *The Peace Hotel jazz band rings in the new year, 1985*

Hamilton House, which the *Shanghai News* reported had been a forbidden place 'under yolk of Anglo-American imperialism,' was crowded with over 1,300 residents.

While the number of visitors fell in the late 1950s, due largely to the hapless devastation of the Great Leap Forward and deteriorating relations with the USSR, the number of Peace Hotel employees rose to around 250. Two notable guests stayed at the hotel in 1960. Field Marshal Viscount Montgomery of Alamein, on his first visit to China in 30 years, came in June 1960 and was reported to have expressed his support for the sovereignty of China over Formosa (Taiwan). Leftist writer and old China hand Edgar Snow also paid a visit. In the early 1960s, one of Snow's long-time acquaintances, premier Zhou Enlai, made efforts to increase diplomatic ties and relations with nations outside the Soviet Bloc, and the Western World was startled by the establishment of diplomatic relations between China and France in early 1964. The negotiations for the agreement, between Zhou and former French premier Edgar Faure, representing President Charles de Gaulles, took place at the hotel in late 1963.

Edgar Faure and his wife meet Zhou Enlai at the Peace Hotel

Visas were easier to come by in 1964 and 1965, and many communist-sympathiser tourists, as well as curious Western businessmen and journalists, made the trip to Shanghai. There were no bars or floorshows, but Sir Victor Sassoon's former suite was on offer for a very modest seven pounds sterling a night. The first group of Western journalists to tour China in this era stayed at the Peace Hotel in May 1964. Andrew Wilson of *The Observer* in London reported that his flight from Shanghai was held up for 15 minutes as C.I.T.S. sought to determine the ownership of an English penny left in a hotel room. He was told by his interpreter that 'nothing is stolen in revolutionary China.' In anticipation of rising visitor numbers, the former Palace Hotel, which had been occupied by the Shanghai Municipal Construction Department since 1952, was converted into the south building of the Peace Hotel and reopened in 1965.

Alas, the flirtation didn't last long and guest numbers plummeted with the advent of the Cultural Revolution in 1966. American labour activist and black radical Vicki Garvine, who moved to Shanghai from Africa on the invitation of the Chinese ambassador to Ghana in 1964, was among the few foreigners working in Shanghai at that time. However, her spell of teaching English language and African-American history at the Shanghai Foreign Languages Institute was truncated, as classes closed and resentment rose, forcing a move to the hotel for her safety. Garvine sighted her English teaching skills on the staff, who, like herself, had plenty of time on their hands. After a stint in Beijing, Garvine returned to the States in 1970, where she continued her career as an influential political activist.

Fortunately the hotel's decorative treasures were also in the safe hands of its staff,

The Dragon and Phoenix Hall in the 1950s.

169

BALLROOM REVIVAL: THE CHINA COAST BALL

When the Mandarin Oriental took over the classic Hotel Bela Vista in Macau in 1990, Ted Marr, a Hong Kong-based Australian lawyer and socialite, was forced to look for a new venue for the society ball he had hitherto organised amidst its colonial splendour. His thoughts drifted northwards to Shanghai and the Peace Hotel. It was with some sentimentality that he took to the seas on the Jinjiang bound for Shanghai in August 1990. The ship, formerly the SS Mariposa, used to carry Australians of his parent's generation on their way to Europe by way of the US overland route, and it was also the well-known namesake of the state-run group that owned the Peace Hotel.

Ted checked in at the newly opened Portman Shangri-La before heading down to the waterfront and his first foretaste of the Peace Hotel. He strolled in and announced, 'look I'm from Hong Kong and I want to do a party for 500 people here . . . and they looked at me quite strangely, because no one had ever said those words in their living memory.' The timing and delivery of his request couldn't have been better. Shanghai was freshly open for business again and the hotel's executives were eager to indulge in their newfound sense of importance. It was the beginning of a relationship that would extend over nine years and bear deliverance of three humungous parties – in 1991, 1992 and 1997, respectively, as well as several smaller ones – the likes of which the city had been starved of for years.

The management preferred to chew over Ted's proposals in what they believed to be the most fitting venue – that of the old Tudor bar on the ground floor of the hotel. Ted recalls his parleys over a beer and peanuts 'sitting cold and shivering in the middle of the day in the thick darkness' of its stone-clad confines. The management's response, however, was much warmer in tone and, from their first nibble, they 'liked the idea though they didn't know what it was going to be.' But, the order for the go-ahead had to come from the lips of the city mayor himself.

Ted 'found ways of doing things' in his dealings with the veteran architects of diplomacy and was forthright in his desire to set a precedent in bringing foreign entertainers up to Shanghai for the party. Cutely, he had introduced the idea by suggesting that 'some of the people in the group would provide entertainment for the others . . . almost like someone getting up at a wedding and singing something.' The entertainers he had in mind were referred to as 'the special Australian dancers who were members of our group' and Ted saw no need to complicate matters by seeking any special permission. The term 'special dancers' soon became a matter of common parlance, as if everybody knew what they were, though nobody really thought to ask. The first clue as to just what Shanghai was getting itself into came at the airport 'when three boys turned up from Sydney with their bags stuffed with frocks, wigs and false boobs.' Officials quizzing them over what was, no doubt, their first ever sighting of such bulbous prosthetics were informed that they were plain old shoulder pads!

It wasn't until the rehearsals, in 'civvies', on the day of the ball that anybody had an inkling as to what was in store. The event was such a sell-out affair that Ted had commandeered the whole of the eighth floor, and in one room a traditional Chinese ensemble, which 'everybody hated,' played a dull prelude to a phenomenal finale. Just as the drag queens had got fully kitted up, photographer David Thurston took them downstairs and immortalised their presence on the Bund. His sensational picture was splashed on the cover of Hong Kong's South China Morning Post magazine. Ted went downstairs to witness a 'mob thing going on as hundreds and hundreds of people appeared out of nowhere.' The ball itself wound up in a more solemn and typically Chinese fashion with a series of speeches on China's opening up to the outside world – and wow, what a flamboyant opening it proved to be. By the time of the next ball the management had become very blasé about the whole affair and they, and particularly their old-time staff, recognised that the days of glitz, glamour and cabaret were right back where they belonged.

'Shanghai-Yaaah!' Cover of the South China Morning Post *magazine, 24 March 1991*

171

who covered them with paper and paint to keep them out of view of the Red Guards. The survival of the dragon and phoenix designs on the eighth floor was a result of their efforts and the hotel suffered little damage during the Cultural Revolution. Staff at the Shanghai Overseas Chinese Hotel, where the only other room featuring such designs was to be found, had not taken such precautions and the room was destroyed.

While guest numbers dwindled, staff numbers rose to around 300 by the end of the 1960s. Those employees who were not sent out to the countryside were given short hours, rolled through political and technical education, and endured endless hours cleaning and re-cleaning the hotel. Many would take 'rests' at home when there was a paucity of guests and be called back in times of need, of which there were few. Mr. Ma Yongzhang, former public relations manager of the Peace Hotel, recalled an instance in 1968 or 1969, when the hotel's solitary foreign guest had 70 staff pandering to him.

Things began to rebound in the early 1970s, as ping pong diplomacy made the headlines and the US table tennis team, who stayed at the Peace Hotel in April 1971, played two exhibition matches to the rapture of confabulatory blue-uniformed crowds. The 15-strong team, along with three American correspondents, were

NOTHING STOLEN

We arrive at the Peace Hotel, formerly the Cathay Hotel, belle of the Orient. Noel Coward wrote 'Private Lives' here. The signs are in Chinese, English and Russian. Each room with twin beds. Clean, but threadbare. Plenty of floorboys and quick laundry service. Poor quality soap. Water tasted of disinfectant but probably just as well. You can leave your door wide open and everything is safe. 'Nothing is stolen in revolutionary China,' my interpreter explains.

William Tuohy,
Los Angeles Times, *5 March 1973*

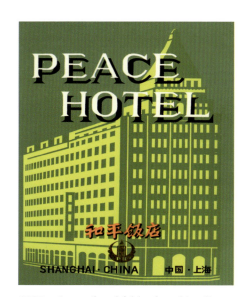
1980s vintage hotel folder found in all guest rooms.

the first US citizens to be admitted as a group to China since 1949. Other teams, including the British, who had finished competing at the World Table Tennis Championships in Japan a week before, also stayed. The event set the arena for President Richard Nixon's historic visit to China in February 1972, when he stayed at the Jin Jiang Hotel, the former Cathay Mansions, and signed the 'Shanghai Communiqué,' laying the path for the normalisation of relations between the two nations. Bilateral ties with the British at the ambassadorial level were agreed upon in the following month and Sri Lankan Prime Minister, Mme. Sirimavi Bandaranaike stayed at the hotel later in the year.

Though the doors of the Peace Hotel had never stopped revolving, it wasn't until the introduction of Deng Xiaoping's open door policy in 1978, that they were opened to all. China was back in business again, 'to get rich [was] glorious,' and the first intrepid, high-spending tour groups from the US and Europe began to arrive in the city once more. Shanghai, like the hotel itself, had been cocooned in a time warp, with heaps of nostalgia in store. Just as in the 1930s, the Peace Hotel, under the aegis of the Jin Jiang Group Holding Company, had little competition from other hotels in the city, and its spirit was revived and imbibed by visitors looking to conjure up the aroma of the 'Paris of the East.' However, faced with the prospect of competition, particularly from emerging foreign joint-venture hotel projects, and a desire to provide more modern facilities for visitors, as well as greater profits, the hotel embarked upon remodelling its rooms and some public spaces in the mid-1980s. In 1985 the hotel's turnover was more than double what it had been in the previous year. Some changes, including the replacement of the original ceiling lights in the Peace Hall with gaudy chandeliers, had already taken place. By 1989 the former eighth-floor lounge had been converted to the Peace Grill, with a faux art deco corridor festooned with imitation Lalique

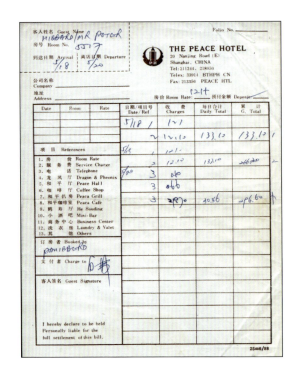

Author's bill for staying at the Peace Hotel in May 1989 with a room rate of just 133 Chinese Yuan a night

plaques on its floor. Much of the original marble panelling on the ground floor had been replaced and furniture that had been kept in the bar was disposed of. Sir Victor Sassoon's personal suite was put to use as a karaoke bar. The hotel was still not yet back in full swing.

The fortunes of the hotel, along with those of the city, began to change in 1990, when Deng Xiaoping gave the green light for Shanghai to hit the big time again. The ambition was to restore its former status as Asia's leading centre for trade, finance and commerce. In anticipation that financiers would again return to the buildings along the Bund, Sir Victor Sassoon's former suite was knocked apart to provide accommodation for a private bankers club in the early 1990s. Along with rising prosperity and greater interaction with the outside world, extravagance and opulence re-entered the city's lexicon. The Most Famous Hotels in the World Organisation of Vienna awarded the Peace Hotel the accolade of 'the most famous hotel in the world' in 1991/92.

The hotel garnered a new sense of self-importance and became a sought after venue for party planners, film producers and fashionistas, as well as for government officials and those still looking to capture the spirit of Old Shanghai. The Peace Hall became the scene of many society events and was used as a set in numerous movies. Parts of Stephen Spielberg's *Empire of the Sun* were filmed in the hotel in 1986 and, amongst other appearances, the hotel later featured in Zhang Yimou's *Shanghai Triad* and Merchant Ivory's *The White Countess*. Parts of the hotel were transformed into an art gallery and showplace for Prada's travelling exhibition 'Waist Down' in May 2005.

Yet, for all the glitz and glamour, age was catching up with the hotel and she appeared as a slender shadow of her former self. With the ambition of resuscitating her prominence and grace, the hotel quietly closed its doors in April 2007. The hotel's south wing, the former Palace Hotel, did likewise, closing a remarkable chapter in the city's modern history. It was a history in which the great men behind the ventures, as well as their guests, invited or uninvited, played a major part.

The hotel's closure came as something of a surprise and shock to its clientele and to the public. A century of international hospitality on the Bund had come to an abrupt end. However, a new era began in 2010 when the two buildings reopened and embarked upon very different new careers. The former Palace Hotel was reborn as the Swatch Art Peace Hotel, with its suites reserved for visiting artists and its public spaces occupied as exhibition and retail spaces, including a range of boutiques on its ground floor displaying the Swatch Group's most prestigious brands. One of Shanghai's most celebrated teatime venues in the 1930s now serves up classic timepieces.

The former Cathay Hotel is once again open to the public as the resplendent Fairmont Peace Hotel, managed by Fairmont Hotels & Resorts. The original ground floor layout of the former Sassoon House has been reinstated, with its series of interlocking shopping arcades revealed for the first time in decades. Etched above the entrance on the Bund, the words 'Sassoon House' have also been restored and the hotel's presidential suite has been named after Sir Victor Sassoon. He may have departed Shanghai long ago, but Sassoon's legacy and vision live on in the hotel in its desire to recapture the spirit of a bygone age when it was the most modern, luxurious and stylish in Asia.

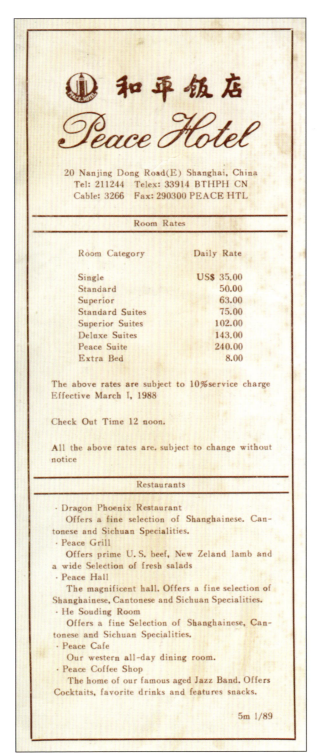

Luxuries on offer at the Peace Hotel, late 1980s

Illuminations on the Bund, 1991

Bund entrance lobby, 1991

Panoramas of the eighth-floor ballroom, lounge and restaurant at the Peace Hotel, 1978

Lobby of the south wing of the Peace Hotel, 1978

Top *Sunny side up, Western breakfast as served in the eighth-floor restaurant, 1978*

Bottom Right *Ceiling light in the Chinese suite, 1990*

Top Centre *Beautifully framed windows in the Dragon and Phoenix restaurant, overlooking the Huangpu River, 1990*

Top *Decorative grille-work in the Chinese suite, 1990*

Bottom Left *Lobby light, 1990*

CATHAY TIDBITS

CATHAY HOTEL ADVICE FOR GUESTS

The Cathay Magazine to be found in all bedrooms offered a few Shanghai DON'TS

Don't trust strangers. The Hotel Office and Enquiry Bureau is a reliable source of information.

Don't make chance enquiries regarding location directions. Ask a Foreign Police Officer if available or consult map at centre page. Failing these, any Foreigner is generally only too willing to point the way.

Don't make trips to the Chinese City, or outside the Settlement or Concession, without a reliable guide. One can be obtained through your Hotel Enquiry Bureau or at most Foreign Motor Garages.

Don't over pay your ricksha coolie. 20 cents Mex. or so is sufficient for most journeys not exceeding ten minutes, Longer runs pro rata.

Don't carry your handbag loosely under the arm; it may be snatched. Carry it in your hand with the strap handle over the wrist.

Don't eat proffered fruits when out walking in the country. The skins of all fruits should be carefully peeled or washed in a weak solution of permanganate.

Don't walk barefooted, not even in your own bedroom, when away from any but the larger Foreign Hotels.

Don't over-tip your Hire-car driver. 20 cents Mex. is correct for journeys up to half an hour.

Don't forget that you are in a Foreign Country. The Chinese are a courteous race and will meet courtesy with courtesy.

Don't travel in the interior without a passport. In some instances a visa is necessary, but a passport often saves an awkward misunderstanding.

Don't eat uncooked vegetables except when offered as American products at Hotels or Cafes of repute.

Don't quarrel with Customs officials; they know their job. Goods purchased in China are now subject to a small export duty.

Don't carry more money than is essential, nor expose, unnecessarily, valuables on your person.

PIDGIN-ENGLISH FOR TOURISTS

Pidgin-English was a unique combination of English or other foreign words within the Chinese idiom. Though the visitor to Shanghai was likely to find English spoken by some of the local population, a far greater proportion could communicate using Pidgin – especially when money was at issue!

For the Cathay Hotel guest the following phrases may have proved invaluable.

I want some tea at once	Catchee tea chop chop
A tip	Kumshaw
Get me some hot water	Pay my hot water
Do you understand?	Savvy?
I want a bath	My wanchee bath
How much is that?	How muchee?
I don't like that	No likee
Is that the lowest price?	No can cuttee?
Is the bargain settled?	Can puttee book?
Do you mean it?	Talkee true?
What do you mean by that?	What fashion?
Can you send this to the Cathay?	Cathay Hotel side can sendee?
That will not do	No can do
How are you? or Good-bye	Chin-chin

183

HOTEL DIRECTORY FOR 1939

SASSOON HOUSE

Ground Floor
Hoggard-Sigler Nichols Rugs
British Flower Shop
Gray's Yellow Lantern Shop
Alexander Clark Co.

First Floor
Dr. A. Renner.
China General Omnibus Co.
Swan, Culbertson & Fritz.

Second Floor
Algar & Co Ld.
RCA Communications Inc.
Mackay Radio & Telegraph Co.
Dr. Ashton Laidlaw
Dr. D. J. Collins
Dr F. B. Hudson
Dr. S. F. Jenson
S. M. Perry & Co.
Dr. P. S. Kawaguchi
Bunge & Co. Ld.
Shanghai Sanitarium Co.
Automatic Electric Sales Co.
Automatic Telephones of China
Employers Liability Insurance, Corp Ld.
Merchants' Marine Insurance Co.
Caledonian Insurance Co.
Shotter, Madar & Co.
American Asiatic Trading Co.
Acme Advertising Agency
Acme Painting & Decorating Co.

Third Floor
E. D. Sassoon & Co.
E. D. Sassoon Banking Co.
Far Eastern Investment Co.
Shanghai Estates & Finance Co.
Shanghai Properties Ld.
Eastern Estates & Land Co.
China Deep Well Drilling
Hamilton Trust Co.
Zikawei Estates Investment Co.
Central Properties
Asian Finance Corp. Ld.
Bombay Trust Corp.
Oriental Investment Co.
Far Eastern Nominees Ld.
Arnhold & Co.
Cathay Land Co.
Metropolitan-Vickers Electrical Export Co.
Henry Simon, Ld.
Textile Machinery Agencies.

CATHAY HOTEL RESIDENTS

Sir Victor Sassoon
Robert Telfer (Manager)
Commander F. R. Davey
W. Warren Sigler
C. D. Hoggard
C. Cavalli
Dr. & Mrs W. S. Parsons
Mr & Mrs Wm. N. Gray, jr.
H. E. Morriss
Wing-Commander & Mrs H. S. Kerby
Judge P. Grant Jones
Mr & Mrs J. E. Hunter
J. T. S. Reed
Mr & Mrs A. M. Wootten
C. F. Thomas
A. U. Fox

THE PALACE HOTEL

Hong Kong & Shanghai Hotels Ld.
G. A. Efron
Bond Street Salon
Readmore Library
S. Nakao

ARCHITECTS AND CONTRACTORS TO SASSOON HOUSE

ARCHITECTS

Messrs PALMER & TURNER
G. L. Wilson, architect. F. J. Barrow,
    engineer.

CONTRACTORS

Building: SIN JIN KEE.
Pile Driving: Messrs HONG KONG
    & EXCAVATION PILE-DRIVING
    CONSTRUCTION Co., Ltd.
Electrical Installation: INNES & RIDDLE
    (China) Ltd.
Plumbing and Heating: SHANGHAI
    WATERWORKS Co., Ltd.
Patent Insulite Flooring: PAUL I. FAGAN
    & Co.
Furniture: WEEKS & Co., ARTS &
    CRAFTS Co., HALL & HOLTZ, TAI
    CHONG.
Doors Frames and Architrave's: CHINA
    WOOD-WORKING & DRY KILN Co.
Sanitary Fittings: DOULTON & SHANK.
Renee Lalique Electric Fixtures: BREEVES
    OF ENGLAND.
Flooring and Joinery: GEORGE McBAIN
    & Co.
Lifts: AMERICAN TRADING Co.

Art Metal Work: SARGENT & POLIS,
    CRITTALL MANUFACTURING Co.,
    ARTS & CRAFTS Co., SOY CHONG.
Shop Fronts: ASIA GLASS Co.
Sprinklers: ARNHOLD & Co., Ltd
Steel Windows: CRITTALL
    MANUFACTURING Co.
Skylights: ALEX MALCOLM.
Tiling and Mosaic: ANDERSEN, MEYER
    & Co., Ltd.
Iron-mongery: ANDERSEN, MEYER &
    Co., Ltd.
Structural Steelwork: DORMAN LONG & Co.
Glass: PILKINGTON Bros. (China) Ltd.
Bronze Canopies: SOY CHUNG.
Copper Lights: PILKINGTON Bros.
    (China) Ltd.
Steel, Bronze and Cast Iron Windows,
Screens for Ground Floor:
    CRITTALL MANUFACTURING Co.
Collapsible Gates: WILLIAM JACKS & Co.
Marble Work: BERTUCCI &
    FINACHIARD
Induroleum Floor to Ground Floor:
    METRPOLITAN CARRIAGE
    WAGON & FINANCE Co., Ltd.
Water-proofing: Messrs ANDERSEN,
    MEYER & Co., Ltd.

BIBLIOGRAPHY

BOOKS

Abend, Hallett. *Tortured China*. Ives Washburn, New York, 1930.

American Women's Club Annual. 1919-1920.

Anon. *All About Shanghai and Environs, The 1934-35 Standard Guide Book*, with a foreword by Peter Hibbard, Earnshaw Books, Hong Kong, 2008.

Anon. "The Shanghai Boom". *Fortune*, Vol. 11, No. 1, January 1935. Time Fortune Corporation, New York.

Auden, W. H. and Isherwood, Christopher. *Journey to a War*. Faber and Faber, London, 1939.

Baker, Barbara. *Shanghai – Electric and Lurid City*. Oxford University Press, 1998.

Barber, Noel. *The Fall of Shanghai* Macmillan London Limited, 1979.

Baum, Vicki. *Shanghai '37*. Oxford University Press, Hong Kong, 1986.

Booker, Edna Lee. *Flight from China*. The Macmillan Company, New York, 1946.

Booker, Edna Lee. *News is My Job: A Correspondent in War-Torn China*. The Macmillan Company, New York, 1949.

Coates, Austin. *China Races*. Oxford University Press, 1983.

Coward, Noel. *Autobiography: Consisting of Present Indicative, Future Indefinite and the Uncompleted Past Conditional* Methuen, London, 1986.

Croke, Vicki Constantine. *The Lady and the Panda*. Random House, New York, 2005.

Crow, Carl. *Handbook for China*. Oxford University Press, Hong Kong, 1984.

Dayo F. Gore, Jeanne Theoharis, Komozi Woodard. *Want to Start a Revolution? Radical Women in the Black Freedom Struggle*. NYU Press, 2009.

Fearn, Anne Walter. *My Days of Strength: An American Woman Doctor's Forty Years in China*. Harrap & Brothers Publishers, New York and London. 1939.

Field, Andrew. *Shanghai's Dancing World* The Chinese University Press, Hong Kong, 2010.

Friedman Marcus, Audrey and Krasno, Rena. *Survival in Shanghai: The Journals of Fred Marcus 1939-49*. Pacific View Press, Berkeley, California, 2008.

Haylen, Lesley. *Chinese Journey: The Republic Revisited*. Angus & Robertson, Sydney, 1959.

Ernest O'Hauser. *Shanghai: City for Sale* Harcourt, Brace, New York, 1940.

Hibbard, Peter. *Beyond Hospitality: The History of The Hongkong and Shanghai Hotels, Limited*. Marshall Cavendish Editions, Singapore, 2010.

Hibbard, Peter. *The Bund Shanghai: China Faces West*. Odyssey Books and Guides, 2007, 2011.

Jackson, Stanley. *The Sassoons*. Heinemann, London, 1968.

Kranzler, David. *Japanese, Nazis and Jews: The Jewish Refugee Community of Shanghai, 1938-1945*. New York: Ktav Publishing House. 1976.

Krasno, Rena. *Strangers Always: A Jewish Family in Wartime Shanghai*. Pacific View Press, Berkeley, 1992.

Macmillan, Allister (ed). *Seaports of The Far East*. W.H. & L. Collingridge, London, 1925.

Meyer, Maisie J. *From the Rivers of Babylon to the Whangpoo, A Century of Sephardi Jewish Life in Shanghai*. University Press of America, Inc., New York, 2003.

Pan, Lynn. *In Search of Old Shanghai*. Joint Publishing Co. Hong Kong, 1982.

Politzer, Eric. "The Changing Face of the Shanghai Bund". *Arts of Asia*, Volume 35, No. 2, March-April 2005.

Robinson, David. *Chaplin, His Life and Art*. Collins, London, 1985.

Roper, May. *China: The Surprising Country*. Heinemann Ltd., London, 1966.

Seagrave, Sterling. *The Soong Dynasty*. Sidgwick & Jackson, London, 1985.

Smith, Whitey with McDermott C.L.

I Didn't Make a Million. Philippine Education Company, Manila, 1956.

Snow, Helen Foster. *My China Years*. Harrap, London, 1984.

T'ang Leang Li (ed). *China Facts and Fancies*. China United Press, Shanghai, 1936.

Tata, S. and McLachan, I. *Shanghai 1949: The End of an Era*. B. T. Batsford, London, 1989.

Train, George F. *The Merchant Abroad in Europe, Asia and Australia*. Sampson Low, Son & Co. New York, 1857.

Wells, Beatrice. *A Visitor to Shanghai in Travel in Vogue*. Da Capo Press Inc., New York, 1983.

Wright, Arnold (ed). *Twentieth Century Impressions of Hongkong, Shanghai & Other Treaty Ports of China*. Lloyds Great Britain Publishing Co., 1908.

NEWSPAPERS AND MAGAZINES

Cathay 1932-1935
China Critic 1930-1936
China Journal 1927-1934
China Press 1911-1948

China Weekly Review (formerly *Millard's Review*) 1917-1949
Israel's Messenger 1925-1930
Los Angeles Times 1937-1974
National Geographic 1933, 1948
North-China Daily News 1865-1949
North-China Herald 1851-1951
Shanghai Evening Courier 1869-1874
Shanghai Evening Post & Mercury 1929-1940
Shanghai Municipal Gazette 1929-1937
Shanghai Sunday Times 1925-1937
Shanghai Times 1925-1942
Shanghai News 1951
Social Shanghai 1907-1912
TIME August 1937
Washington Post 1937 -1972

ARCHIVES

McBain family, provided by Niall McBain.
Memoirs of Isabel Duck, Imperial War Museum, London.
National Archives, London.
Personal interviews with Peace Hotel staff, 1989 and 1991.
Public Records Office, Hong Kong.
North-China Hong List Shanghai, 1872-1947.
Royal Institute of British Architects, London.
SOAS, University of London.
Shanghai Municipal Council Reports, Gazettes, Secretariat and Public Works Department Files. Shanghai Municipal Archives.
Teeside Archives.
Victoria Sharonova collection on Victor Podgoursky

PHOTO CREDITS

All images from the collection of Peter Hibbard, apart from: American Express: 100. Barnes family: 36. British Steel Archive Project, with the permission of Teesside Archives: 40 (ID: 26756), 43 (left. ID: 26759), (right ID: 26755), 70 (bottom left, ID 26764; bottom right, ID 26762). Magnus Bartlett: 167 (top), 178, 179, 180 (left). Dennis George Crow: 15. Michelle Garnaut: 95. HBA: 169. Elizabeth Jennings: 37 (top left), 39. Lafuente Family Archives, facilitated by Alvaro Leonardo: 27, 80 (bottom). Ma Yongzhang (Fairmont Peace Hotel): 155, 167 (bottom), 168. Hugues Martin: 46 (left), 78 (top). Eric Niderost: 63 (top), 69, 71 (middle & bottom), 72, 73 (left), 106, 107. Shanghai Municipal Archives: 158 (left), 159 (right), 160, 161, 164 (top & bottom), South China Morning Post: 171. Upton Sino-Forum Archive: 62, 118 (top), 145. The images used in this book from the Upton Sino-Forum Archive (USFA) have been provided with the permission of Steve Upton for use under applicable laws.